American Indians and the Market Economy, 1775–1850

Edited by
Lance Greene and Mark R. Plane

Foreword by Timothy K. Perttula

THE UNIVERSITY OF ALABAMA PRESS
Tuscaloosa

Copyright © 2010
The University of Alabama Press
Tuscaloosa, Alabama 35487-0380
All rights reserved
Manufactured in the United States of America

Typeface: AGaramond

∞

The paper on which this book is printed meets the minimum requirements of American National Standard for Information Sciences—Permanence of Paper for Printed Library Materials, ANSI Z39.48-1984.

Library of Congress Cataloging-in-Publication Data

American Indians and the market economy, 1775–1850 / edited by Lance Greene and Mark R. Plane ; foreword by Timothy K. Perttula.
   p. cm.
   Includes bibliographical references and index.
   ISBN 978-0-8173-1714-0 (cloth : alk. paper) — ISBN 978-0-8173-5626-2 (pbk. : alk. paper) — ISBN 978-0-8173-8479-1 (electronic) 1. Indians of North America—Material culture. 2. Indians of North America—Ethnic identity. 3. Indians of North America—Economic conditions—18th century. 4. Indians of North America—Economic conditions—19th century. 5. Economic anthropology—United States. I. Greene, Lance, 1963– II. Plane, Mark R., 1964–
   E98.M34A45 2010
   305.897—dc22
                                                                                               2010026333

Contents

List of Figures and Tables   vii

Foreword
Timothy K. Pertulla   ix

Acknowledgments   xiii

Introduction
Lance Greene and Mark R. Plane   1

1. "These Indians Appear to Be Wealthy": Economy and Identity during the Late Fur-Trade Period in the Lower Great Lakes
Michael Strezewski   19

2. "Remarkable Elasticity of Character": Colonial Discourse, the Market Economy, and Catawba Itinerancy, 1770–1820
Mark R. Plane   33

3. Identity in a Post-Removal Cherokee Household, 1838–50
Lance Greene   53

4. Business in the Hinterlands: The Impact of the Market Economy on the West-Central Great Plains at the Turn of the 19th Century
Cody Newton   67

5. Negotiating Borders: The Southern Caddo and Their Relationships with Colonial Governments in East Texas
P. Shawn Marceaux and Timothy K. Perttula   80

References   99

Contributors   127

Index   129

Figures and Tables

FIGURES

1.1. Map of Indiana   20

1.2. Weight of chinking fragments (in grams) recovered from 1-meter subunits in Block 1; location of subsurface features and hypothesized structural outlines within Block 1   24

1.3. Stone pipe manufactured in the style of a white clay pipe   30

2.1. Digital reconstructions of common Catawba vessel forms   41

2.2. Polygonal soup plate with edge decoration   43

2.3. Percentages of kaolin pipe fragments recovered at Catawba town sites   45

3.1. Location of study area in southwestern North Carolina   54

3.2. Substructure cellar pit excavation at the Welch site   60

3.3. Chlorite-schist pipe from the Welch site   64

4.1. Location of Lykins Valley   71

4.2. Lykins Valley site excavation block   74

4.3. Rock art panel from 5LR293 based on image in Morris et al. (1979:89)   78

5.1. The distribution of Hasinai, Kadohadacho, and Natchitoches groups and other related tribes   81

5.2. Historic Caddo archaeological sites and phases in east Texas   90

5.3. Late-18th- and early-19th-century Spanish ranchos and the locations of aboriginal groups around the Pueblo of Nacogdoches in east Texas   93

TABLES

3.1. Minimum number of ceramic vessels by decorative style, Welch site   61

4.1. Exploration into the Great Plains region   69

4.2. Known Indian groups in the Lykins Valley vicinity   70

4.3. Post-contact radiocarbon dates and isotopic data from the Lykins Valley site   72

5.1. Historical context and events in Caddo and colonial history   82

5.2. Caddo populations through the colonial era   84

Foreword

The chapters in this volume began as presentations at a 2007 Society for American Archaeology (SAA) meeting held in Austin, Texas. The challenge posed to the presenters—now authors—was to begin with a consideration of case-specific studies of Indian groups adapting/responding to the changing world (i.e., market economy or what constituted a market economy in different North American locales at specific times) between 1775 and 1850, but still maintaining their Indian group identity. The social, economic, and demographic realities of that changing world for Indian groups led to the second challenge: characterizing the diversity of adaptations and significance of Indian ethnic identity as expressed in archaeological, ethnohistorical, and historical/archival research.

It was my opinion at the time of the meetings that the papers were remarkably cohesive for a symposium at the SAA—illustrating the diversity of Indian adaptations in an increasingly hostile and marginalized world, as well as the scope of adaptive changes among these groups at different times and places and different geopolitical realities. The papers then were, and book chapters now are, continental in scope, ranging from the Carolinas in the East, Indiana in the Midwest, Texas in the near Southwest, and Colorado in the near West. Virtually all of them share an approach that looks at agency, individual choices, and practices among different Indian groups. The authors then employ that approach in using a nuanced perspective on material culture to tease out strategies and responses—some successful, some not—by Indian groups that are not necessarily apparent from either just archaeological or historical records, but that are synthetic in perspective.

Acculturative models and simple dichotomous models of culture contact and change play little part in these book chapters, and that is a positive step forward in presenting a more refined understanding of late-18th- to mid-19th-century life ways of American Indian groups. It is an impressive Indian history that is being offered here, one that archaeology is uniquely equipped to study, once a nuanced appreciation of the meaning of material culture items and subsistence practices can be brought into play. Late-18th- to mid-19th-century American Indian groups had artifacts of European American manufacture and artifacts made from European American raw materials, but that does not tell the whole story. Ultimately, the reader will come away with a clearer view of the realities of culture contact between Indian groups and the British, American, French, and Spanish colonizers.

The book chapters fall neatly into two groups, regionally and geopolitically, based on the contexts in which culture contacts and the burgeoning colonial and increasingly international market economy played out for Indian groups between 1775 and 1850. First are those groups living among Europeans in 1775, these being among the many groups living in eastern North America that had experienced long and sustained contact and commercial trade with the British and Americans (e.g., Calloway 2003; Rothschild 2003): the Catawba and Cherokee (in this case, a post-Removal Cherokee group in North Carolina). A second set of Indian groups were still living on the frontier in 1775, and they outnumbered Europeans; the market economy revolved around the fur trade and other less expansive commercial economic developments (e.g., the horse trade among the Caddo) (see Usner 1992), represented here by the Wea around the Great Lakes—in a frontier area contested by the British and Americans—the Caddo in east Texas, and unidentified groups in north-central Colorado. The Caddo lived in an area contested between the French and Spanish, and then the Spanish and Americans, and then between Mexicans and Texans (Smith 2005). The diversity in kinds of contact and geopolitical settings in the late 18th through early 19th centuries in these different parts of North America has consequent effects on the adaptive possibilities of Indian groups as well as the character of the archaeological and historical records.

American Indian groups such as the Wea and the Caddo, among many others, recognized the advantages of the fur trade for their own purposes and reaped the benefits (i.e., access to goods and gifts), at least for a time. The fur trade from an Indian perspective was not just a market or consumer pursuit: it played a key role in traditional practices surrounding the kin-based exchange of gifts. Unfortunately, these Indian groups were situated between two worlds and two or more colonial powers, and eventually they paid the price because of their support of one colonial power against another. Land-hungry Americans rolled over these American Indian groups, and most were eventually removed to the West, to Indian Territory.

European goods on Indian sites are oft times more revealing about gift exchanges and Indian social relationships (within an Indian community and among different Indian groups) than they are about participation in market economies or as evidence of the adoption of functionally mundane commodities. It is important to look beyond the obvious, to refocus on what European goods may reveal about Indian practices and strategies from a perspective that emphasizes local actions and beliefs for their explanatory power. Archaeologists must be fully cognizant of how these material culture items were produced and used.

A key observation raised by several authors in this volume is the importance of food remains from historic archaeological contexts—and the culinary traditions that generated them—in the appreciation and grasping of Indian cultural identities. For truly, the materials associated with dining are easier to change than what was being consumed, and what was being consumed maintained a strong Indian character despite changes in land use and subsistence practices in a world of new religious forces, land base reductions (cf. Rothschild 2003:94), and a host of other economic, political, and social events. Looking at subsistence in this manner is a means to explain transformations in American Indian cultural landscapes as they struggled to keep (but mainly lost) a secure land base.

Another key point that resonates throughout the chapters is how material culture (whatever the source) comes to have particular meanings and plays certain roles among Indian groups that strengthen identity and cultural survival, and need not imply a dilution of Indian cultural practices. The authors contribute insights into the contexts in which there are multiple relationships at work between Indian groups and colonial governments and market economies. It is in their attempts to emphasize the negotiated character of Indian consumer practices and adaptive strategies that the reader will come away with a better appreciation of how important individual actions and practices are in archaeological studies of the post-contact period—when they can be perceived—if we are to fully appreciate how Indian groups maintained their identities and survived as groups and communities in hostile and marginalized environments. Archaeological and documentary records thus show the engagement of Indian groups in determining their own fate.

Timothy K. Perttula

Acknowledgments

This volume originated from a symposium at the 2007 meeting of the SAA. That symposium enabled us to meet a wonderful group of researchers who share our interest in American Indian identity during the market era. The success of that session prompted us to take the next step and seek publication of the papers presented.

Having finally arrived at our goal, we would like to thank our authors, not only for their fine chapters, but also for their patience and perseverance in seeing this project through to completion. Neither of us had edited anything of this magnitude. We can only say that your forbearance is greatly appreciated, and we hope that our work as editors does justice to your contributions.

We would also like to offer heartfelt thanks to the staff at The University of Alabama Press. Their enthusiasm for this volume has meant a lot to us, and their skillful shepherding is what ultimately made the whole thing possible.

Lance Greene and Mark R. Plane

American Indians and the Market Economy, 1775–1850

Introduction
Lance Greene and Mark R. Plane

This volume seeks to extend the discussion of Indian people incorporated, willingly or not, into the market economy in America between 1775 and 1850. Indian individuals and groups attempted to adapt to the changing economic and political world while maintaining both cultural identity and group cohesion. Their adaptations were complex and varied; locale informed the range of available options. Indians had some choices, but within contexts of unequal power relations. Historical archaeology is uniquely suited to study the impacts of the market economy, which changed the production, distribution, and consumption of material goods throughout North America.

Indian Removal has tended to dominate discussions of Indians after the Revolutionary War, particularly the Cherokee "Trail of Tears." This event is often associated with imagery of a "vanishing race" ill equipped to deal with economic modernization, inevitably marginalized both socially and economically, and finally destroyed by westward expansion of settlers and industry. A major goal of this volume is to challenge this limited portrait of Indian societies and to demonstrate the degree to which Indians were able to actively participate in modernization. For example, Cherokees in North Carolina commonly farmed and ran livestock on plantations and were renowned for their road-building skills, while Catawbas in backcountry South Carolina leased their reservation land to white tenant farmers, allowing many members of the tribe to travel to Charleston to sell handmade ceramics and other goods at market.

Indians had long engaged in the selective adoption of European goods and foods, often reworking material culture physically or socially into their own economic systems. A common reaction to the market economy was the commoditization of craft items such as baskets, pipes, and pottery. In this maneuver, Indians strategically selected and modified elements of their own culture to fit within European American social and economic structures. Study of the changes in the production and use of these items, from household items to market commodities, elucidates the changing role and effect of the market on Indian groups.

American Indians continued to wield political power as well. The Caddo of eastern Texas used both their land base and their position in the "middle ground" to extract land rights and annuities from the United States. The Creek, Chickasaw, Choctaw, and Cherokee lands in the southeastern United States were not surrendered until the 1830s. Until that time, these lands were terra incognita as far as the federal government was concerned: unmapped, they contained no private property boundaries, and the people within these boundaries were not subject to federal censuses, taxes, or military service. Even after the removal of the bulk of their populations, small numbers of many of these tribes remained in their homeland and maintained traditional communities for decades. Members of the Welch family acted as patrons for one of these communities and helped maintain a traditional Cherokee town for two decades after Removal.

Some changes were relatively gradual, as with the Kiowa, Arapahoe, and Cheyenne groups in north-central Colorado. Although whites did not traverse the area until well into the 19th century, these Indian groups acquired numerous European goods, while maintaining a largely traditional subsistence. Other groups were affected by more rapid, and often violent, transformations. The Wea and Kickapoo had engaged in a lucrative fur trade with British and French traders in the town of Kethtippecanunk (Indiana), until its complete destruction by the Kentucky militia in 1791. Almost a half century later, the Cherokee (and numerous other tribes) were recovering from the effects of military occupation and forced emigration.

The social and political impact of American Indians during this era was significant but has been largely overlooked. Historians, writing after the "closing of the West" and throughout the 20th century, created a national perception of the disappearance of Indians after the founding of the United States; episodes of Indian loss and victimization such as Indian Removal have been used to reinforce this perception. This literature tends to hide the reality of frequent encounters between Indians and U.S. citizens during the late 18th and early 19th centuries. Conn (2004:3) asserts that the "near-constant physical presence" of American Indians caused European Americans to raise moral and ethical questions regarding Indian origins, abilities, and rights. In this volume, we attempt to demonstrate that American Indian participation was a significant aspect of the market revolution in America.

Indians negotiated the expanding market economy during the late 18th century and the first half of the 19th century through practices such as the creation and maintenance of markets for the sale of craft items, the selective acceptance of European goods and foods, and the maintenance of tribal lands. Increasing exposure to the market and to whites during this period elicited responses that usually involved the acceptance of certain European practices, but also a strong desire to maintain traditional communities and identities.

Geographically, the chapters in this volume focus largely on Indian groups east of the Mississippi River, the region representing the greatest population growth and market expansion during the study period. Areas include the Catawba River Valley in South Carolina and the southern Appalachian Mountains of North Carolina to the Wabash River Valley of central Indiana. Two of the chapters focus on areas west of the Mississippi River—eastern Texas and northern Colorado—and show how Indian groups were affected in these regions.

We begin the Introduction with a discussion of the growth of the market economy during the study era, followed by a look at changes in American historical archaeological research, beginning in the 1960s. In the section American Indian Identity and Market Economics, we briefly discuss the radically different forms of political economy between American Indian and European groups during the contact era. We then discuss in more detail commodities, processes of exchange, the creation of value, and the social ramifications of these economic forms and processes. In the section Race, Ethnicity, and American Indian Identity, we focus on how Indian groups chose to classify themselves, and how these definitions were challenged by the social, political, and economic changes of the period. Following a discussion of race and ethnicity is an overview of the chapters in this volume and their investigation of and contribution to its major themes. Each is a case study of a particular Indian group and their reactions to changes wrought by the market. These local histories, in succession, illustrate the range of impacts and responses by small communities across a large portion of the United States.

Growth of the Market Economy, 1775–1850

We adopt Stokes's (1996:1) definition of the market economy as an economic system in which "farmers and manufacturers produced food and goods for the cash rewards of an often distant marketplace," in contrast to the earlier "largely subsistence economy of small farms and tiny workshops, satisfying mostly local needs through barter and exchange." In the past 20 years, many historians have discussed what has been called the "market revolution," beginning in America in the late 18th or early 19th century (Sellers 1991; Stokes 1996). This market revolution expanded at different rates across different parts of the United States, leaving people in some regions mostly involved in local production and trade until the mid 19th century (Stokes 1996:11). This shift in economic exchange affected all aspects of life for those involved, both at the household level and in terms of broader social ties.

The growth of the market economy occurred through population expansion, technological innovation, infrastructural development, and political support, creating qualitative changes in everyday life that have lasted to the present day. The

75-year span, 1775–1850, involved dramatic social and economic changes for the vast majority of people in the United States. Major trends included rapid population growth and westward expansion, as enormous numbers of European immigrants quickly moved away from the eastern seaboard. Land grants provided to Revolutionary War veterans and the Louisiana Purchase ensured an adequate land base for the steady movement of populations into western territories. Technological advances in different regions of the United States dramatically expanded the market economy. The improvement of the cotton gin by Eli Whitney in 1793 was the basis for an increasing slave population (Watson 1996:49). Construction of water-powered textile mills in New England, also beginning in the last decade of the 18th century, would soon be responsible for processing a large portion of the cotton produced by enslaved African American labor in the southern states.

The market revolution gained force in 1815, as President Madison and the Republican-controlled Congress provided critical support to industry and commerce (Sellers 1991:70–79). State and federal governments began encouraging infrastructural development, and corporate charters were granted for the development of turnpikes, railroads, bridges, plank roads, and canals (Stokes 1996:2). Large-scale improvements in infrastructure, such as the Erie Canal, completed in 1825, sparked a transportation boom, allowing settlers to move westward across the midwestern plains. These projects magnified profits from crops and livestock by providing viable, inexpensive transportation to markets in the East. The continual expansion of people and markets westward during this period culminated in the ideology of Manifest Destiny, a term coined in 1845.

In the United States, state power increasingly supported the market and industrialization (Clark 1996:35–37). State support of these institutions coincided with the development of stronger and more formal uses of state power, including a greatly increased military presence and a greater reliance on controlling the land and people through the creation of detailed property and census data (Anderson 1991; Calhoun 1994).

As historians have documented, and as the authors in the present volume illustrate, the impact of the market economy occurred at different rates and in different forms in the various regions of the United States. In the North, the market economy was expanding rapidly by 1800. During the first decades of the 19th century, the market revolution for much of the population entailed a series of transitions, from home production (e.g., piecework for both men and women) to a workforce incorporated more fully into an industrialized setting (Clark 1996). In the South, lowland cotton plantation owners embraced the market economy, while farmers in the piedmont and mountain regions were largely isolated from intensive market participation. This "dual economy" was characteristic of the region until the Civil War (Watson 1996).

The market economy did cause some overarching changes in all regions. Increased mobility of individuals and families occurred early. As these changes continued and broadened, community-wide impacts deepened; community ties were weakened as individuals and whole families departed to follow labor opportunities (Clark 1996:34; Stokes 1996:3). Market and industrial expansion also enabled broad participation in a wider material culture, as increasing arrays of consumer goods became available to more segments of the American populace. Thus, by the early 19th century, goods such as matched sets of dishes and tea sets had become popular with all but the poorest households (Deetz 1996; Goodwin 1999; Leone et al. 1987).

American Indian life was affected by all of these changes, and various forms of market participation sprang up throughout the United States. Power relations between governments and Indian people shifted dramatically from the colonial period to the 19th century. Indians found themselves in a new environment as the political scene shifted away from colonial struggles between three superpowers. Although the British, French, and Spanish continued their colonial pursuits during this era, the main political and military power was the United States, bent on expansion of population and trade (Silliman 2005:58–59). As Silliman observed, "shifts from colonial to postcolonial periods can bring about changes not only in administrative and governmental control but also in indigenous experiences, opportunities, and constraints in a system of domination" (2005:59).

Of course, Indian groups continued to deal with many of the old threats, such as encroaching white settlements. Now, within the new state, they also had to deal with new problems, such as expanding mercantilism, federal and state laws, changing gender roles, changing racist ideologies, economic marginalization, dispossession, and increasingly unequal power relations (Silliman 2005:59).

Recently authors have debated treating colonialism and postcolonialism as separate processes (Gosden 2001; we discuss postcolonialism as both a historical epoch or process and, later in this chapter, as a theoretical perspective). Although historians end the colonial period in 1776, the Spanish and French carried on colonial pursuits, and the United States continued certain aspects of the colonial project, leading some researchers to refer to American colonialism. Acts of oppression, marginalization, and racism obviously existed during both eras. Additionally, the expansion of national boundaries for the United States spans from 1776 through 1959, making temporal definitions of the colonial and postcolonial eras extremely difficult. Nevertheless, substantial changes in governmental structures and economic systems did occur between the two eras. These distinctions must be considered to investigate fully the impact on Indian groups during each era. As Lightfoot writes, "While there is a plethora of excellent studies on the archaeology of urbanism and capitalism, immigrant communities, and ranching and mining technology in the western United States, Indian peoples comprise only a minor component of this research, if they are present at all. In contrast to the wealth of information on indigenous encounters with European explorers and colonists, Native peoples essentially disappear from the archaeological literature with the advent of American colonialism" (2006:282).

Indian groups, no longer in the position to play colonial powers against one another, became subject to the increasing desire for land and market growth. In addition, market expansion during this era was inextricably tied to race. Historians and historical archaeologists have produced detailed research on the massive expansion of African American slavery in the southern United States (e.g., Genovese 1965; Otto 1984; Singleton 1985). In contrast, the effects of hardened racist ideologies on Indian people have rarely been addressed. This does not mean that Indian groups became powerless under these stricter controls. Indians found numerous ways to negotiate the new political terrain, including participating in the burgeoning market, as some had done in the colonial era. They also resisted in a variety of ways.

Historical Archaeology

During much of the 20th century, historical archaeology in the United States focused on famous personages and elites, or the earliest European settlements (e.g., Cotter 1958; Harrington 1952; Harrington et al. 1956; Noël Hume 1982). In the late 1960s, Charles Fairbanks began investigating African American slave sites (Ascher and Fairbanks 1971). This research initiated the field of plantation archaeology, focused on illustrating the lives of slaves (e.g., Adams and Boling 1989; Otto 1984; Singleton 1980, 1985; Wheaton et al. 1983). In a broader sense, it initiated the study in historical archaeology in America of "those of little note" (Scott 1994).

Even after Fairbanks began this research, there continued in historical archaeology in the United States a bipartite periodization of research interests and goals. The first period spanned roughly from initial European contact through the American Revolution. The second spanned from the end of the Revolutionary War through the late 19th century. These periods were tied to popular perceptions regarding the old colonial era and the new, or modern, national era. The underlying tenets of the first period (1492–1783) were the struggle between European superpowers and the significant role played by American Indians. Models of acculturation applied to Indian groups measured—through material culture—the impact on traditional cultural, political, and religious life. Indians were seen as maintaining a certain amount of power, through their control of the "middle ground" (White 1991), and commodities such as deerskins, and their ability to serve on the frontlines of combat. They were often portrayed as determinedly maintaining cultural identities in the face of an onslaught of European power.

The foundational concepts of the second era (1784–1900) included race slavery, industrialization, urbanization, and capitalism. In the 1970s and 1980s these concepts were increasingly applied to "those of little note," including African American slaves on southern plantations and whites involved in wage labor and life in urban and industrial settings (e.g., Beaudry and Mrozowski 1988; Branstner and Martin 1987; De Cunzo 1987; Singleton 1980, 1985). However, Indians remained largely neglected. The reasons for this erasure were manifold. The "death" of the American Indian and the westward march of progress or Manifest Destiny have been defining moments in American historical thought. Indians were considered inseparable from the frontier, and as that frontier moved westward, it was understood that Indians followed.

Archaeological investigations of Indian groups during this era assumed the association of these groups with the dying frontier, not as participants in the modern nation-state and market economy. This symbolic death of the Indian was seen as the loss of tribal power in American affairs, and perhaps even the loss of "Indianness," as Indian people were seen as being forced onto reservation lands where they supposedly surrendered their cultural traditions and all but ceased to exist. Like many such popular perceptions, this was incorporated into academic thought and research. While perhaps not overtly racist, the removal of American Indians from the entire history of "modern" America nonetheless served to perpetuate racist stereotypes of Indians.

By the early 1990s, historical archaeology stood at the forefront of many new research paradigms: interpretive, contextual, urban, household, and feminist approaches. These bodies of literature spanned numerous and varied theoretical and methodological approaches and opened the door for more sophisticated and nuanced studies. Research into African American life revealed oppressive power structures and varied forms of resistance to them (Epperson 1999; Mullins 1999; Singleton 1996, 2004; Singleton and Bograd 1995; Wilkie 2000). Investigations of factory environments highlighted daily resistance to dangerous and degrading working and living conditions (Beaudry and Mrozowski 2001; Leone 1999; Mrozowski et al. 1996; Shackel 1996). They helped set the stage for the historical archaeology of American Indians, including discussions of culture contact versus colonialism, acculturation and Indian agency, and postcolonialism.

Since the mid-1990s these issues have been openly addressed in the literature (Gosden 2004; Lightfoot 1995; Scott 1994; Silliman 2005, 2006). For example, Stephen Silliman (2005:55–57) argues against conflating colonialism and "culture contact." In his view, "culture contact" and "contact period" are under-theorized terms that downplay the often profoundly inequitable nature of interactions between Europeans and American Indians, as well as the length of time involved in these interactions and extent of changes that occurred among Indian groups. Moreover, Silliman notes that culture contact fails to convey the same political charge as colonialism for Indian descendent communities, and given that archaeology traces its own heritage in colonialism, this political dimension should resonate for archaeologists as well.

Discussions of colonialism and its tremendous impact on indigenous populations must be tempered with recognition of the agency of colonial subjects. Acculturation was not an inevitable result of colonialism; cultural change was by no means a uniform process of transformation from Indian to European. Thus, Lightfoot (1995:206–207) forcefully argued that simplistic approaches to cultural change deny the agency of American Indians and ignore their efforts at resistance or strategic engagement with European colonial powers. Indeed, Lightfoot (1995: 206) cautions "that the adoption and use of new technologies and materials in colonial frontiers were complex processes involving various economic, political, ideological, and engendered considerations, and that native peoples were active participants in selecting or modifying new artifact forms. New cultural traits were adopted, modified, and created to fit within the underlying ideological structures of both non-European and European peoples." This process is particularly evident in frontier situations.

In this discussion, it is important to understand the nature of human agency and its limits. Wilkie and Bartoy (2000:748–749) suggest an approach in which people are "conscious of the system in which they live and capable, within its structural constraints, of pursuing alternative avenues of action." Within this approach, individuals are not "radically independent agents," but are instead "situated within a web of social relations that define their position in society." Nevertheless, individuals and groups may envision themselves in ways that "manipulate and challenge" the inherent tensions in society, thereby constructing and pursuing their own agendas.

With these understandings, even the broad adoption of European culture cannot necessarily be taken as indicating a lack of agency or the loss of Indian identity. For example, in his work on Removal Period Cherokee communities in North Carolina, Brett Riggs (1999) describes the development of two distinct socioeconomic classes among the Cherokees. He documents the so-called mixed-blood or *métis* families, who spoke English, embraced the market economy and many aspects of Western material culture, and were considered the "intelligent and wealthy class." They are contrasted with the culturally conservative "fullbloods." Denigrated by white observers as "backward," "indolent," and "ignorant," fullbloods engaged primarily in subsistence farming and possessed very little in the way of mass-produced commercial goods. While each group clung tenaciously to Cherokee identity, they diverged significantly in their conception of what it meant to be Cherokee, pursuing radically different economic strategies, lifestyles, and political agendas. Far from being forced to adopt Western culture and ideology, *métis* individuals strategically utilized the latter to redefine the relationship between European American society and the Cherokee Nation, seeking to compete with whites on their own terms (see Greene, this volume).

This discussion of Indian agency highlights the importance of local histories in explorations of colonial and postcolonial eras. In the development of archaeological perspectives on these eras, world systems and postcolonial theories have both been highly influential (Gosden 2004:7). The world systems approach offers a world-historical view that is very useful in the identification of long-term trends. While this long view is part of the very raison d'être of archaeology, it is not necessarily conducive to identifying and explicating subtle variation in the archaeological record. Postcolonial theory offers a complementary perspective, focusing on the local rather than the global, on the contingent rather than the inevitable, and on the agency of the colonized rather than the power flowing from imperial centers (Gosden 2004:7).

Focusing on local histories is important for two reasons. First, there are important differences in the exercise of colonial power, both between and within empires (Gosden 2004:18–19). Thus, in comparing the Russian and Spanish colonies in 19th-century California, Lightfoot (2005) describes distinct "enculturation programs," noting how that of the Russians at Fort Ross was relatively hands-off compared to the Spanish missions to the south.

In addition, there is no one-size-fits-all approach to addressing the reactions of marginalized people. Different settings, opportunities, actors, motivations, and choices produce a plethora of responses, from co-option and collaboration to subtle subversion and armed resistance (Gosden 2004:18–19). One of the major goals of this volume is to further examine this range of variation, both in terms of the exercise of colonial and state power and the range of Indian responses.

American Indian Identity and Market Economics

Investigations of the impact of colonial and state power structures on American Indians can illuminate how Indian communities survived and maintained, or lost, cultural or group identity. One of the challenges faced by the authors in this volume was reconciling the transformational power of the market economy with the agency of individuals on the one hand, and the influence of indigenous values and patterns of culture within Indian societies on the other. In *A New Order of Things*, Claudio Saunt (1999:1–2) describes the degree to which European conceptions of "order and things, power and property" overturned Indian lives in the decades following the American Revolution: "Before the Revolution, Creeks did not strive to accumulate significant amounts of material possessions or to protect and defend their belongings from their neighbors. Yet by the 1810s, a few people had thousands of dollars and hundreds of cattle and slaves. The kind as well as the quantity of these new possessions reshaped the lives of Creeks."

The changes described by Saunt are of course related to broad sociopolitical differences between European and American Indian societies. When Europeans arrived in eastern North America, they encountered radically different forms of political economy and personal identity. In stark contrast to the European colonial powers, Indian societies lacked stratified classes, full-scale administrative bureaucracies, and pervasive socioeconomic inequality. While Indian polities did possess elites in the form of chiefs, and differences in status and wealth existed between elites and commoners, they nevertheless lacked the degree of economic differentiation that accompanies capitalist production, and the political differentiation accompanying state-vested authority. Indian economies were instead firmly grounded in communal, domestic, and local production, with even family members of elites undertaking the normal range of productive activities. Indian politics were grounded in consensus rather than decree (Muller 1997:41–46, 83–107).

While European economies extolled the primacy of the individual and the accumulation of personal wealth, the corporate kin group, reciprocity, and gift exchange were major organizing principles in Indian economies. For example, under the traditional Harmony Ethic of Cherokee society, the individual was sublimated to the corporate group, with assertiveness and competition within the group negatively sanctioned. Institutionalized hospitality and generosity served as economic leveling mechanisms, while inordinate personal accumulation of wealth was seen as representing a serious character defect (Thomas 1958).

As our title suggests, many of the chapters deal with large-scale effects of the market economy on American Indian societies. However, the authors are as often concerned with small-scale analyses; for example, examining the changing nature of particular classes of goods, or obtaining household-level perspectives on material culture and everyday life within this "new order of things."

The order of things, their uses and meanings, is bound up in questions of identity and cultural context. Whether in terms of gender, race, and class, or sacred and profane space, culturally constructed understandings of who and where people are influence the quantity and quality of the things they use, how those things are obtained, the uses to which they are put, and the meanings with which they are inscribed. Thus, in this volume, American Indian identity and the market economy is not merely a convenient rubric, but rather describes a necessary connection between particular people and things in particular historical and cultural contexts. Moreover, given the ability of historical archaeologists to richly contextualize material culture using documentary evidence, exploring this connection is all the more imperative.

Although the phrase "market economy" suggests an economic focus for this volume, the connection between things, identity, and cultural context blurs the boundary between social life and the supposedly distinct realm of commerce. In his introduction to *The Social Lives of Things,* Arjun Appadurai (1986:13) very broadly defines commodities as objects whose socially relevant feature is exchangeability for some other object (whether in the past, present, or future). This definition greatly expands the range of societies in which some form of commodities occur, rendering the process of commoditization a matter of degrees rather than presence or absence.

Focusing on the importance of the movement of things through different cultural milieus, Appadurai (1986:3–4) argues that rather than the value of commodities conditioning economic exchange, processes of exchange in fact create the value attached to commodities, and that politics (broadly construed) creates the link between exchange and value. In this view, value is not an inherent property of objects, but is a judgment made about them by subjects who desire them (Simmel 1978); this desire, though, is "a socially regulated and generated impulse," not the isolated product of "individual whims or needs" (Appadurai 1986:52). Finally, it is important to recognize that economic objects circulate in different regimes of value in space and time (Appadurai 1986:4). As objects move from one cultural context to another, their function, meaning, and value may change dramatically; moreover, this movement itself may impact an object's value.

This discussion highlights the fact that objects are not exchanged in cultural, political, and historical vacuums. Questions regarding an object's origins, its previous owners, its current owner's social status and role in that object's social trajectory will factor in any estimation of meaning or value. Therefore, we emphasize the degree to which the value and meaning of objects is a function of identity as well as cultural context of exchange or consumption, since things themselves often symbolize cultural identities, and identity greatly determines what things one desires, one's ability to satisfy those desires through exchange (i.e., degree of agency), and the understandings, expectations, and calculations of other parties involved in the exchange and consumption of goods. It is thus within a very complex social dialectic that even the most utilitarian of commodities may obtain significant meaning and value (see Plane, this volume).

Within this theoretical framework, Indian crafts produced for trade are commodities, not relics representing people and ethnic traditions frozen in time. Nevertheless, in addition to being commodities, such objects may serve as important markers of identity and Indian "tradition" to both producers and consumers, reflecting the degree to which discourses on identity function within processes of exchange, imbuing objects with meaning and value. Thus, commodities representing Indian identity not only generated income for their Indian makers and sellers, but also played an important role in identity formation, for both American Indians and white citizens of the new American Republic (Deloria 1998; Raibmon 2005). Indians used these objects to survive culturally and carve a niche for themselves within the new economy (Raibmon 2005). However, through such objects (and other means) white Americans expressed romantic, enlightenment notions of the ancient or colonial past and tapped into popular conceptions of Indian liberty and communalism in order to distance themselves from the entrenched classism of European societies and celebrate Republican ideals (Deloria 1998).

Within anthropology, gift exchange has traditionally been viewed as representing the antithesis of commodity exchange, with gift exchange tending to link things more closely to persons than commodity exchange, and to more deeply "embed the flow of things in the flow of social relations" (Appadurai 1986:11). Gifts are seen as expressions of reciprocity, sociability, and spontaneity, whereas commodities represent profiteering, self-centeredness, and scheming (Appadurai 1986:11–12).

Anthropologists have more recently emphasized the economic aspects of gift exchange in small-scale societies, revealing the strategies, calculations, and self-aggrandizement that underlie transactions often portrayed as purely social in nature (Bourdieu 1977:171). Another important consideration is the social and political nature of commodity consumption, which is often portrayed as merely a result of economic processes. Thus, Douglas and Isherwood (1996:vii–ix) argue against abstracting commodity consumption from the social process, of viewing it as merely the result or objective of work. They also inveigh against reductionist economic theories that limit consumption only to satisfying material or psychic welfare and urges toward competitive display.

Consumer goods render cultural categories visible and stable, and function as necessary mediating material in social life, especially in constructing, maintaining, and gaining access to social networks (Douglas and Isherwood 1996:vii–ix, 38, 61–63). Identity, politics, and value are intimately linked within this framework, as assemblages of goods make visible statements about the hierarchy of values to which those who obtain them subscribe. In the dialogue about value that occurs in the process of consumption, goods in an assemblage present sets of meanings. In addition to their practical uses, consumer goods enable people to engage with others in a series of social exchanges with significant economic and political dimensions (Douglas and Isherwood 1996:xxi).

The consumption of goods, that is, their use beyond commerce, often involves economic and political considerations, as goods in social life represent information systems that people seek to control. Those who can control that information often seek to restrict access, striving for "monopoly advantage," erecting barriers to entry, consolidating control of consumption opportunities and practicing techniques of exclusion. Those excluded must either consolidate around remaining consumption opportunities, perhaps redefining the meanings of various goods in the process (see Plane's interpretation, this volume, of the meaning of imported European ceramics in Catawba households), or seek to infiltrate monopolistic barriers to social networks (Douglas and Isherwood 1996:62–63). Politics, identity, and the value and meaning of things are thus linked both inside and outside the marketplace. Social exchanges involve economic motivations, while social forces motivate economic behavior (see Plane, this volume, on the social dimensions of the sale of Indian pipes and pots in the marketplace, or the purchasing of such "curios" by European travelers).

Race, Ethnicity, and American Indian Identity

In his work on race and racialization in America, Orser (2007:8–9) distinguishes race from ethnicity on the basis of self-ascription. Racial categorization creates relatively large agglomerations of people on the basis of real and perceived physical differences (and often cultural attributes as well) and is imposed from the outside by people who classify themselves as belonging to a different racial group. In contrast, ethnic affiliation is self-imposed from the inside; perceived cultural commonality is the basis for ethnicity.

While this is a useful distinction, race and ethnicity also share certain important features. Racial and ethnic groupings may endure as cultural entities over very long periods of time. Race and ethnicity are also elastic and dynamic cultural constructs that may vary and change according to the needs of groups and individuals. The existence of either type of grouping depends upon the maintenance of social boundaries. Although ethnic and racial boundaries entail insiders and outsiders, both people and cultural information will inevitably traverse these lines (see Strezewski, this volume). Nevertheless, increasing cultural similarities between interacting ethnic or racial groups do not correlate in any simple way with a reduction in the social relevance of their identities (see Barth 1969 on ethnic boundaries). And while race is a historical phenomenon related to European exploration and colonization and racial classification has often been an instrument for domination (Orser 2007:9), ethnicity is no less suitable for political purposes.

The archaeological investigation of ethnicity has largely become the province of historical archaeology (Jones 1999). Indeed, Bruce Trigger (1995:277) went so far as stating that ethnicity is a subjective phenomenon that cannot be studied archaeologically without relevant historical or ethnographic data. Whether or not this should be so is perhaps debatable; nevertheless, recent ethnographic and ethnoarchaeological research on identity has prompted archaeologists to exercise caution when using stylistic differences in material culture assemblages to identify distinct ethnic groups (Hegmon 1998:266; see Newton, this volume).

Following Barth (1969:11, 13–14), we define ethnic groups as social constructs that provide ascriptive and exclusive membership to a cultural identity group, with actors using ethnic identity as a basis for interactions with others. Ethnic identities involve interrelating cultural characteristics, although these may change over time. Within ethnic groups, some characteristics may be used by individuals as signals and emblems of cultural difference, while others may be ignored; in some circumstances, radical differences between actors may actually be downplayed or even denied (Barth 1969:14). Thus, there will be variation between ethnic group members, with some showing many and some showing relatively few of the group's recognized characteristics (Barth 1969:29). Such was the case on Welch's farm, as described by Greene in this volume, as Cherokees constructed a community in which a façade of Western culture concealed complex negotiations involving race, class, gender, and ethnicity.

Interacting ethnic and racial groups often strive to define themselves in opposition to one another. This is particularly important in which groups compete for social and economic resources, resulting in the construction of "insider" and "outsider" categories. Indeed, ethnic or racial identities may develop and become elaborated as "insiders" and "outsiders" engage in a dialectical process of defining themselves in opposition to one another (Lincoln 1989:7–8; Weber 1968:341–342).

This dialectic is often skewed in favor of a dominant social group. When backed by the power of nation-states, dominant social groups may be successful in limiting the social and economic opportunities of those who are excluded, and highly influential in defining their identities as well. Within such institutional and discursive constraints, the identities and lifestyles of outsider groups may ultimately become dependent upon the definition imposed by the dominant group; out of economic and social necessity, outsiders begin to live in ways that fulfill ethnic or racial stereotypes (Fanon 1968). The latter points are particularly relevant in terms of the relative importance and functions of ethnicity among Indian groups (see Greene, Plane, this volume).

Barth's work has proved useful to a wide variety of anthropologists interested in grappling with the complexities of cultural boundaries, although, due to the variability of human behavior, even among living peoples ethnicity can be difficult to analyze (Banks 1996; Orser 2004). These difficulties have been compounded by theoretical debates over the objective grounding for subjective claims of ethnic identity; the most prominent models in these debates have been primordialism and instrumentalism.

Within primordialism, ethnicity is seen as a culturally constructed extension of biological kinship (Keyes 1981:5–6). Primordialist theory posits that groups construct ethnic identity in terms of those elements of culture that most fundamentally define their identity, specifically, narratives relating to common descent and ancestral homelands (see, e.g., Hall 1997), expressed in discourses (*sensu* Barthes 1993) such as religious rituals, national histories, and origin myths (Bentley 1987:26; see Marceaux and Perttula, this volume).

Instrumentalism views human action as rational and goal oriented; within this model, ethnic identity is a political strategy through which interest groups pursue collective advantage (the same may be said for racial identity as well). According to instrumentalists, since ethnic identity is founded on rational self-interest, the emotional power of ethnic affinities lies in its potential to advance shared interests

(Bentley 1987:26). Authors in this volume demonstrate the tension between the pull of primordial attachments and necessities of survival in the market economy (see Marceaux and Perttula).

Chapters in This Volume

The following chapters reveal a set of common goals for the Indian groups represented: simultaneously adapting to the new political terrain while attempting to maintain cultural identity and group cohesion. The diverse research also demonstrates the significance of studying local responses to market developments, as the chapters in this volume illustrate that Indian groups both incorporated aspects of the market economy and associated goods into their own social and economic systems, *and* adapted various aspects of Indian culture to fit within the market economy.

We hope that this work reveals the significance and appropriateness of local histories regarding the archaeological and historical investigation of Indian people during this era. These chapters together show the ability of historical archaeology, through the thoughtful use of archaeological and landscape data, the archives, and oral histories, to "defamiliarize" (Tarlow 1999) the past in regard to American Indians in the market economy and to illustrate that Indian people in the United States during the early Federal period actively participated in, and sometimes fought against, the market economy in a variety of ways.

The movement of people and information across ethnic boundaries is well illustrated in the chapter by Michael Strezewski. Excavations at the late-18th-century fur-trading post and Wea village of Kethtippecanunk revealed a mixture of Wea and French *Canadien* material culture. Both French and American Indian artifacts were recovered from the foundations of two houses built using French-style *pièces-sur-pièces* timber construction. Between the two sets of structural remains was a circular tuber-roasting pit; Indian groups throughout the region used such rock-filled roasting pits. This and other material evidence of a multiethnic occupation shows the potential ambiguity or hybridity of ethnic identities when groups choose to share food, clothing, and shelter. While racial and ethnic classifications were used to create lines of division, these boundaries were often crossed. The Wea chose to participate in the profitable deerskin trade and in the creation of a hybridized community in which everyday life involved an amalgamation of Indian and non-Indian practices and material culture.

In his chapter, Mark R. Plane describes the dialectical nature of identity formation between Catawba Indians and whites in South Carolina. During the 18th century, the Catawba were important military allies of South Carolina, buffering the colony from the French and their Indian allies and in turn becoming favored partners in the lucrative deerskin trade. During this time, documentary evidence suggests that both the British and Catawbas considered martial prowess and ferocity in battle as defining elements of Catawba identity, characteristics that fit with European racial discourse on the aggressive, warlike nature of savages. Of course, warfare, hunting, and exchange were activities fully in keeping with traditional men's roles in Indian society, but under colonialism, they were conducted within a radically different political economy.

With the end of colonial-era warfare and the deerskin trade, the Catawbas shifted to an itinerant lifestyle. Within this new economic strategy, pottery and pipes produced for trade by Catawba women became an important symbol of Catawba identity. The Catawbas' itinerancy and their low-fired, handmade earthenware readily meshed with European discourse on primitive, nomadic savages. It is also likely that as the new public face of Catawba identity, the nonthreatening, romantic savagery embodied by women potters possessed more commercial viability within the market economy than that of male hunter-warriors.

The pottery and pipes made by Catawba women generated income that helped Catawbas to survive economically. What is perhaps more significant about these ceramics is the way in which their exchange and use values were directly tied to the identities of both their Indian makers and European American buyers. Economizing was certainly a factor for many consumers in the purchase of utilitarian objects such as colonoware vessels and pipes. However, romantic images of the wild savage and vanishing race, nostalgia for the colonial past, and demand for curio-goods, fueled by enlightenment notions of intellectual or scientific curiosity, also influenced European's desire for "authentic" Indian crafts. For Indian groups such as the Catawba, the production and sale of such goods were critical to maintaining group identity and a connection to the past, representing a process of "crafting tradition and continuity through repeated and contested use" of cultural forms (Raibmon 2005:12), with Indians restaging and reinscribing the past using available forms and within existing cultural contexts (Bhabha 1994:3).

Lance Greene investigates the reestablishment of a traditional Cherokee community in the mountains of North Carolina immediately after the Cherokee Removal. His archaeological research focuses on an intermarried Cherokee/white couple, John and Betty Welch, who supported this Cherokee community. Through the purchase of a large block of land after Removal, the family created a space for such a community to be reestablished. The plantation deed was held by Betty Welch, the only white person in the family. The economic and political power she wielded as a married woman was almost unheard of in southern white society but was not so radical in Cherokee society, in which women held various roles of power. For more than a decade, the Welches maintained the façade of a southern plantation, a disguise for a different kind of community residing in the background.

The Welch family embraced certain aspects of Western culture, such as the accumulation of considerable personal wealth, including the ownership of African American slaves. The Welches engaged in market-oriented agricultural production, constructing their identity using a wide array of Western material goods; however, they were very selective in the Western goods they chose; for example, rejecting the most expensive porcelain tablewares in favor of relatively "utilitarian" whitewares. The Welches needed to achieve a certain level of consumption in order to maintain appearances in Anglo society as freeholders with certain rights and privileges. Yet as a mixed-race household, the Welches were effectively barred from participation in the "consumption opportunities" of wealthy Anglo society, obviating the need for the most elegant tablewares. At the same time, the accumulation and display of wealth beyond a certain threshold had the potential to alienate the Welches from the traditional Cherokees who labored on their farm. In this community, individual consumption was strictly limited by a strong corporate ethos and a worldview of limited good. In negotiating the competing demands of very different consumption regimes, the Welches strategically rejected the standards of wealthy Anglos and held fast to traditional Cherokee governing structures of the local community.

The adoption and modification of new materials to fit within traditional modes of practice is examined by Cody Newton in his chapter in this volume. The Lykins Valley site in northern Colorado was probably occupied by a coalescent group of members of various Plains tribes, a response to European disease. Although disease caused a demographic shift, European materials acquired by these groups were incorporated within Indian modes of technology, exchange, and production. The Lykins Valley during the late 18th and early 19th centuries offered opportunities for hunting bison and other game, but also for acquiring trade goods from outlets to the north and south. Although the Indians had access to a variety of European tools, they continued to use stone tools produced from local and nonlocal raw materials. The presence of arrow points illustrates the continued use of the bow and arrow, and lithic endscrapers and ground stone reveal the use and maintenance of a multifaceted stone-tool technology on site. The similarities between the assemblage from the Lykins Valley site and other equestrian Plains Indian sites from the period suggest similar adaptations to living on the peripheries of an expanding market economy; a mixture of traditional and European technologies, in conjunction with evidence of traditional subsistence patterns, suggests these groups maintained significant continuity in cultural practices prior to sustained contact.

Newton hesitates in assigning ethnicity to the occupants of the Lykins Valley site, noting the high level of mobility among Indian groups in his study region and their tendency to amalgamate and absorb Indian refugees as means of surviving European expansion and epidemic disease. He also calls attention to the homogeneity of material culture assemblages among Plains equestrian groups, spotlighting how material culture traits may crosscut ethnic boundaries.

Marceaux and Perttula demonstrate the importance of primordial narratives in their chapter on the historic Caddo. Historic accounts indicate that the southern

Caddo were organized into three loosely affiliated, probably kin-related groups. These groups were each attached to sacred homelands until a 1780s disease epidemic took the lives of two-thirds of all the Caddo. This event, combined with threats from Eastern tribes forced westward, led one Caddo group, the Kadohadacho, to abandon the homeland of their ancestors, and coalesce with other Caddo groups as a means of survival. The consolidated Caddo tribe renamed their new home after the first village of all Caddo peoples noted in origin stories. The loss of population led to an inability to defend themselves against external threats, so Caddo subgroups were forced to amalgamate. In order to facilitate this process and create an inclusive Caddo identity, they simply shifted the historical focus of their origin stories to emphasize their common roots and downplay cultural differences when naming their new settlement.

Conclusion

This volume fills a gap in American historical archaeology of the post–Revolutionary War period. Research of this period has included the archaeology of African American slaves, urban wage laborers, and rural whites; only recently have the lives of American Indians been addressed. With this volume, we hope to continue this direction in archaeological research.

The following chapters begin to illustrate the diverse ways in which Indian groups adapted to the market and struggled to maintain group identity: through occupation, ownership, and leasing of land, the production and sale of commodities (sometimes involving co-option of "noble savage" imagery), conglomeration and ethnogenesis, and when possible, outright avoidance of the larger impacts of the market. As research in historical archaeology moves to address the "diversity, adaptability, and autonomy of local forms of culture, and the agency of indigenous peoples" (Lydon 2006:306), the significance and distinctiveness of these local histories become more apparent. The chapters in this volume amply demonstrate the importance of exploring local reactions to the development of the market economy and the often-central role of material culture in this complex historical process.

1 / "These Indians Appear to Be Wealthy"
Economy and Identity during the Late Fur-Trade Period in the Lower Great Lakes

Michael Strezewski

Introduction

Beginning in the 17th century, a unique melding of American Indian and French culture was created in the context of the Great Lakes fur trade (White 1991). Though Indian cultures were being transformed via contact with Europeans, their manufactured goods, and the fur-trade economy, French *Canadiens* living deep within Indian lands also changed their way of life, both economically and practically. Archaeological data from these sites provide a unique opportunity to assess change, continuity, and identity within a colonial context (e.g., Nassaney 2008; Tanner 1987).

In the late 18th century, the town of Kethtippecanunk was the hub of Indian and European American fur trading in the central Wabash River Valley and was occupied by Wea Indians and a number of fur traders who lived in their midst. The town was approximately 15 kilometers northeast of present-day Lafayette, Indiana, at the confluence of the Wabash and Tippecanoe rivers (see Figure 1.1), and is presently part of Prophetstown State Park.

Despite its historical significance and potential for documenting questions of cultural identity (from both the Indian and French perspectives), contemporary descriptions of the town are few and do not provide much information regarding such matters as the town's spatial extent, the density of the occupation, and whether or not the two ethnic groups were segregated or intermixed. Although site 12-T-59 had been identified as the town of Kethtippecanunk in the 1970s, prior to recent investigations by the Indiana University–Purdue University Archaeological Survey (IPFW-AS) (Strezewski et al. 2006, 2007) archaeological work at the site had

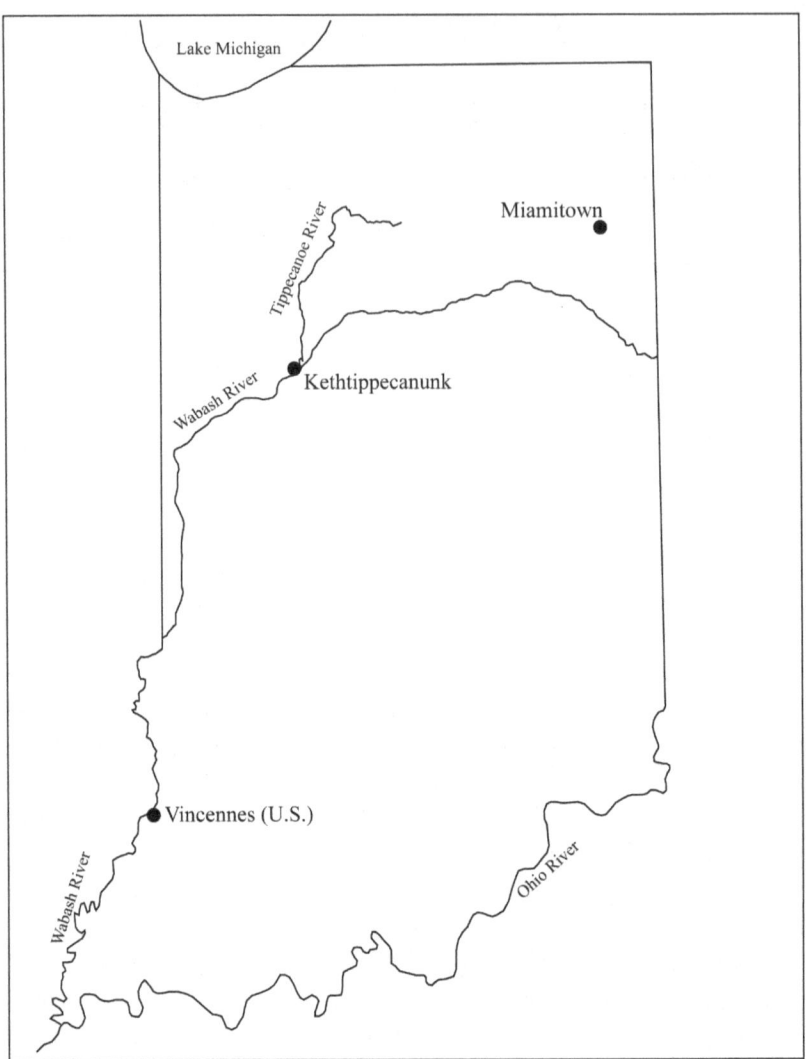

1.1. Map of Indiana, showing locations mentioned in the text

been of short duration and limited scope (e.g., Dobbs 1975; Trubowitz 1992a). Our research goals over two field seasons have been to gain a basic understanding of the site via shovel testing, extensive geophysical investigations (magnetometry and resistivity), and targeted excavations. Our work at Kethtippecanunk has provided details on the daily lives of the town's residents and has given valuable insight into the cultural change and continuity from both the French and American Indian perspectives.

Historical Background

Kethtippecanunk had been occupied by the Wea since at least 1733, when a village named "Kiepigono" is mentioned in reference to a smallpox epidemic that was sweeping the region at the time (Michigan Pioneer and Historical Society 1905: 108–109). For most of its existence, it appears that the town was a purely Indian habitation site. By the time of its destruction in 1791, however, Kethtippecanunk also had a resident population of ethnically French fur traders (Quaife 1921:330–331). Though documentary sources are sparse, evidence suggests that the traders did not move to the town until the 1780s, possibly having migrated from Fort Ouiatenon, which had been built in 1717 as an entrepôt for the fur trade. By 1774 the fort was described as "a miserable stockade surrounding a dozen miserable cabins" (Krauskopf 1955:157) and this extreme state of disrepair may have been the impetus for traders to establish a new base of operations a short distance upriver.

With the 1783 Treaty of Paris, which ended the Revolutionary War, the lower Great Lakes were formally incorporated into the territory of the United States. The U.S. claim to this area, however, was on paper only, and the British continued to occupy posts within American territory. The British also maintained alliances and trading relationships with the Wabash River Indians (i.e., the Wea, Piankashaw, Kickapoo, and Mascouten), who, as a result, were mostly pro-British (Wheeler-Voegelin et al. 1974; White 1991:399–400, 434). Part of the reason for the continued British presence was the profitable fur trade. Although the fur trade in the lower Great Lakes was on the decline by the last decade of the 18th century, fur exports out of Montreal still amounted to roughly £200,000 annually, with one-half of this amount derived from the Upper Mississippi Valley and Great Lakes (Sleeper-Smith 2001:74; White 1991:481).

To the south, along the Ohio River, large numbers of American settlers were pouring into the region. The non-Indian population of Kentucky had gone from fewer than 1,000 in 1780 to nearly 75,000 ten years later (McBride et al. 1996: 191). The American population at Vincennes, which since 1733 had been ethnically French, had risen dramatically as well, as more Americans moved into the region (Barnhart and Riker 1971:255). Indian peoples of the Wabash Valley reacted to the pressure of increasing numbers of land-hungry white settlers by launching frequent raids into Kentucky and along the Ohio River (Barnhart and Riker 1971:246). Although many settlers were killed, a secondary focus of these raids was to destroy the settlers' economic base, in the hopes that they would leave. Horses and merchandise were frequently stolen, and livestock were killed. Boats traveling on the Ohio River were also attacked and ransacked (Bergmann 2005:26–27). Violence between American Indians and American settlers brought U.S. resentment to a head in the early 1790s. Indian groups were aware of the potential destruction that might be brought down upon them as a result of these attacks, and feared American reprisals (Cunningham 1967:45, 47).

As a result of Indian depredations and the perceived complicity of the French and British traders, Secretary of War Henry Knox authorized a punitive expedition against the towns of the Wabash. Brigadier General Charles Scott raised 900 Kentucky militia and proceeded to the central Wabash Valley with the express purpose of destroying Indian towns and capturing as many women and children as possible. These hostages were to be held in American hands until the Indians agreed to peaceable relations with the United States (American State Papers, Indian Affairs 1832–1834:I:129–130).

On June 1, 1791, Scott's force attacked and burned the Wea, Kickapoo, and Mascouten towns located in the vicinity of the former site of Fort Ouiatenon. The next day 360 of the men under Lieutenant Colonel James Wilkinson were dispatched to destroy the nearby town of Kethtippecanunk. Wilkinson's force lay in wait until 4:30 in the morning on June 3, at which point he attacked, catching them completely by surprise. After a short fight, the town's inhabitants fled across the Tippecanoe River, and Kethtippecanunk was burned to the ground.

The traders as well as the Indian peoples within the town suffered the wrath of the Kentucky militia. The aggression against the fur traders was likely due to the fact that it was widely believed that they were encouraging Indian violence at the behest of British government representatives in Detroit (American State Papers, Indian Affairs 1832–1834:I:96; Quaife 1921:301). Scott, in fact, presented his evidence for this suspicion in his official report to Congress. He asserted that "many of the inhabitants [of Kethtippecanunk] were French, and lived in a state of civilization; by the books, letters, and other documents, found there, it is evident that place was in close contact with, and dependent upon, Detroit" (American State Papers, Indian Affairs 1832–1834:I:131).

According to eyewitness accounts, Kethtippecanunk was quite impressive for a frontier settlement. One anonymous soldier from Wilkinson's expedition described it thus: "This town . . . contained about 120 houses, 80 of which were shingle roofed . . . ; the best houses belonged to French traders, whose gardens and improvements round the town were truly delightful, and every thing considered, not a little wonderful; there was a tavern, with cellars, bar, public, and private rooms; and the whole marked a considerable share of order, and no small degree of civilization" (Imlay 1916:12).

William Clark, later co-leader of the Lewis and Clark expedition, was also present during the attack and provides other details about life at Kethtippecanunk. His journal entry for that day mentions that the expedition burned 70 houses, 30 or 40 of which had shingle roofs. Other items destroyed during the attack included 1,000 bushels of corn, bear's oil, plows, carts, salt, cattle, and hogs. Notably, Clark also indicated that "these Indians appear to be wealthy," suggesting that he was impressed by the town and the quantity of material goods and livestock they encountered (Draper Manuscripts 1949:63J:141). Scott himself described Kethtippecanunk as "the most important settlement in that quarter of the federal territory" (American State Papers, Indian Affairs 1832–1834:I:131).

Archaeological Investigations

Archaeological investigations at Kethtippecanunk were conducted in 2005 and 2006. Work initially focused on identifying the extent of the 18th-century component as well as several prehistoric components. Investigations at Kethtippecanunk consisted of shovel probe survey and wide-interval magnetometry, which were used to identify those areas with the greatest concentrations of 18th-century materials and provide a rough idea of overall artifact density. Three excavation blocks were opened to test areas of the site that contained evidence for 18th-century habitation. The largest of these, Block 1, was a 65 m² unit placed over an area identified via magnetometry and test excavations as a probable trader's structure or structures (see Figure 1.2). Two intact subsurface features were identified within the block. The first of these was a rectangular subfloor storage pit containing large quantities of burned structural materials, chinking, and domestic debris.

The second of the two features was a circular pit 1.5 meters in diameter. Excavation revealed that it was lined with wood charcoal and filled with approximately 680 kg of fire-cracked river cobbles. Based on ethnohistoric and archaeological evidence, this feature likely represents an Indian-style pit used for roasting tubers.

Though the majority of the artifacts from Block 1 was identified in the plowzone, the excavation of the entire area in 1.0 m² subunits provided a means of generating distribution maps that aided in interpreting the activities that occurred within its limits. Using these maps (particularly those showing the distribution of burned chinking, window glass, hand-wrought nails, and limestone fragments), we have been able to tentatively identify the presence of two structures. Although no structural foundations were identified, pieces of dressed limestone, indicating a possible foundation, were noted in the plowzone.

Based on archaeological and historic data, it is likely that the structures identified at Kethtippecanunk were of *pièces-sur-pièces* construction, a French building technique common to the region (Mann 2008). *Pièces-sur-pièces* structures consisted of a wooden frame of squared vertical timbers with horizontal beams that were then inserted between the vertical posts. The structural elements were held together by means of a system of grooves and tongues (Gauthier-Larouche 1974; Moogk 1975). Late-18th- and early-19th-century ethnic French in the Detroit area (and those areas influenced by Detroit) often built their structures in this manner (Au 1995). At least one early-19th-century trader's structure in neighboring Warren County was likely *pièces-sur-pièces,* confirming the use of this construction

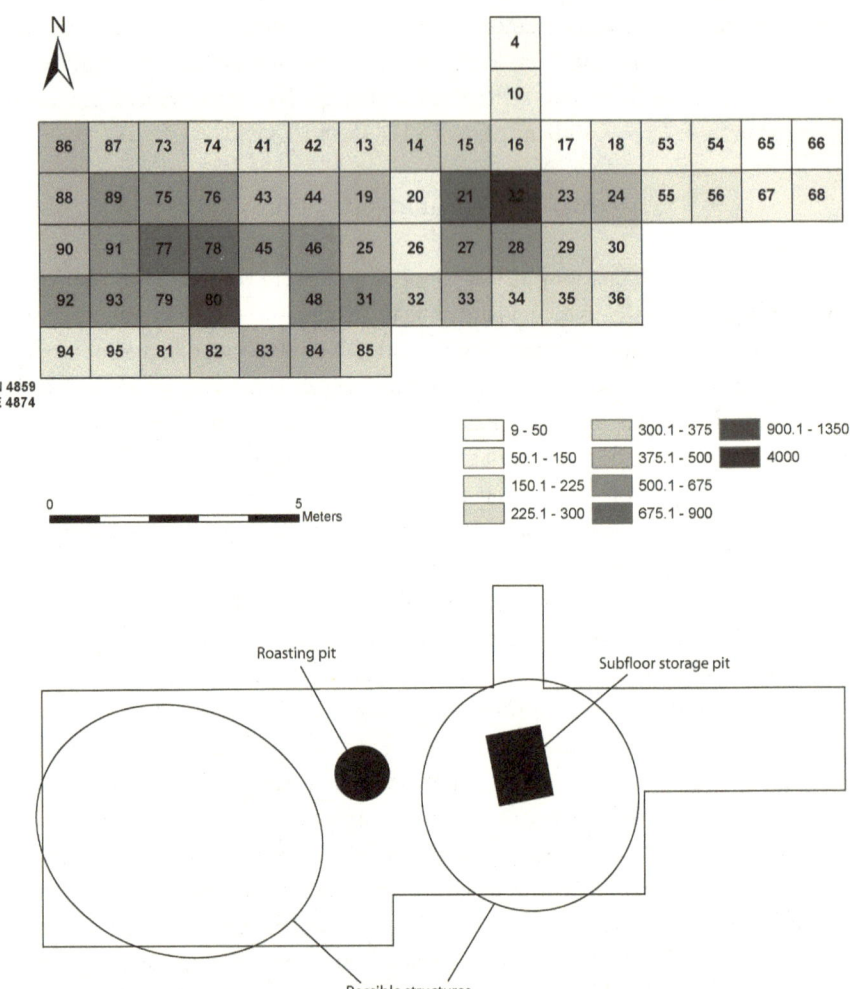

1.2. Weight of chinking fragments (in grams) recovered from 1-meter subunits in Block 1 *(top)*; location of subsurface features and hypothesized structural outlines within Block 1 *(bottom)*

technique in the area (Mann 2008). From an archaeological perspective, structures of this type would likely leave little or no subsurface evidence of their wall outlines, since they were most often constructed upon a limestone foundation. Other evidence for the substantial, European-style nature of the Block 1 structures is the presence of large quantities of window glass, nails, and structural hardware. Building materials were likely brought up river from Vincennes or down from Detroit— no small feat considering Kethtippecanunk was a frontier settlement at some distance from these main supply sources.

Excavations in two other areas of the site failed to recover 18th-century remains in primary context. Block 2, at the northern edge of the site, contained additional 18th-century artifacts. However, these were confined to a secondarily deposited plowzone and had likely been transported from slightly upslope. Nonetheless, the presence of chinking, nails, and window glass in Block 2 indicates that a substantial structure stood near this spot. Excavations in Block 3 identified three prehistoric features, but no evidence of 18th-century occupation was noted.

Overall, the assemblage from Kethtippecanunk indicates the clear presence of both Indian peoples and the traders who lived in their midst. Picking apart the two assemblages, however, is a difficult task. With few exceptions, by the end of the 18th century, there was a great deal of Indian/non-Indian overlap in material culture as Indian peoples abandoned many of their traditional industries in favor of European manufactured goods such as metal tools and cooking pots (Wagner et al. 2001). Readily identifiable artifacts of Indian manufacture were most often those for which a European analog was not available. These include items such as stone pipes (used in religious ceremonies; see Trubowitz 1992b), iron, brass, and silver tinkling cones, and brass fragments manufactured into arrow points. All these items were recovered during our investigations. However, it must be acknowledged that cultural exchange also occurred in the other direction. French traders, especially those who lived and worked in close proximity to Indian peoples, often adopted aspects of Indian clothing and adornment (Nassaney 2008:315). Given this fact, even items like tinkling cones cannot be definitively attributed to an American Indian presence at Kethtippecanunk. Within a long-standing multiethnic community like Kethtippecanunk, terms like "French" and "Indian" lose their meaning, due to the considerable degree of cultural crossover (Nassaney 2008:311).

Not surprisingly, there is no indication of "Indian" versus "non-Indian" areas within any of the excavation blocks and items of possible Indian manufacture are found within areas in which the European-style structures were likely located. For this reason, much of the Kethtippecanunk assemblage must be treated as the mixed remains of the two ethnic groups occupying the site. Although this fact limits the interpretive ability of the assemblage to some degree, there are still a number of interesting patterns that provide information regarding the economic activities and identity formation within and between these two groups.

The Kethtippecanunk Economy

The nature of exchange within the fur-trade economy was fundamentally different for European traders and American Indians. Indian peoples saw the act of trading skins for manufactured goods within the framework of a traditional kin-based exchange of gifts. In this way of understanding exchange, labor was mobilized via access to social networks, thereby creating a system of rights and obligations between two parties (Wolf 1982:90–96). The understanding, then, was that each party would satisfy the needs of the other out of a sense of duty to one's "kin" (White 1991:129). In order to establish trading relationships, fictive kinships were created with particular traders, often times through smoking rituals (Mann 2004). In some cases, kin relations were more than fictive, as French (and later, British) traders intermarried with Indian women (Peterson 1981:121–123; Sleeper-Smith 2001), thereby tapping into the kin networks of the trader's spouse (Wolf 1982:91). Under this system, many British traders who had not established kin relationships via intermarriage found it quite difficult to get a foothold in the fur trade (Sleeper-Smith 2001:57). With the de-emphasis of the profit motive in favor of a kin-based mode of production (at least from the Indian point of view), a "straightforward domination" of the local village by the market did not occur (White 1991:95). Trade had been, to a great extent, conducted on Indian terms.

From the point of view of the traders (and their suppliers in British-controlled Detroit), the situation in the Wabash Valley was a different one. Fur traders and the merchants that supplied their goods were in the business of turning a profit. To that end, fur traders had to get the most favorable exchange rates from their Indian clients and minimize gift giving (Rogers 1990:63). These objectives were the antithesis of the Indian manner of exchange; fur traders attempted to find a means of negotiating these two economic worlds. Though some traders were able to accomplish this, indications are that many were not.

The traders and Indian residents of Kethtippecanunk were likely engaged in the market economy in other ways. Sleeper-Smith (2001:74–75) has noted that many of the residents of fur-trade communities grew agricultural products for profit, supplying fur traders, soldiers, and other nonagricultural members of society. When the fur trade lagged due to war or poor harvests, agricultural pursuits served as an "economic safety network" for towns like Kethtippecanunk (Sleeper-Smith 2001:74). The presence of plows, livestock, and large quantities of agricultural produce at Kethtippecanunk (Draper Manuscripts 1949:63J:141) indicates that the town was probably a source of foodstuffs for the region. Since Indians did not readily take to using European-style plows, it is most likely that the presence of this item at Kethtippecanunk is related to agricultural production by fur traders and their families. Because horticulture was traditionally a woman's activity among Indian peoples of the Great Lakes, Indian women would have played an important role in this aspect of the economy. Agricultural production could be a valuable addition to the household income (Sleeper-Smith 2001). The importance of agriculture to Kethtippecanunk's economy is underscored by a quote from Wilkinson, who returned to the former town site two months after its initial destruction to disperse the Indians once again. He remarked that "after the destruction of this town, in June last, the enemy had returned and cultivated their corn and pulses, which I found in high perfection" (Smith 1882:II:237). Wilkinson also remarked that the amount of corn grown around Kethtippecanunk was "in much greater quantity than at l'Anguille," referring to the Indian town of Kenapacomaqua on the Eel River (Smith 1882:II:237).

Although the British-controlled fur-trade economy had survived the Revolutionary War, American efforts to bring the Great Lakes area under their political and economic control made a continued British presence far from certain. William Burnett, a trader in the nearby St. Joseph River Valley noted in February 1791 that "we are all in a very precarious situation at present with respect to those that has any property in this Country. I am afraid that I will have much to do to make ends meet this year" (Cunningham 1967:45). Prices for furs were low and many of the Detroit-based merchants who were supplying trade goods were in financial dire straits (Quaife 1928:226, 235, 253, 273, 426, 480). One major supplier, John Askin, remarked in 1793 that "the Indian Trade alone in its present State affords a poor livelyhood for any person" (Quaife 1928:480). At least some of these financial woes can be attributed to a decrease in the amount of time Indians spent on hunting and trapping while they were away attacking American settlers to the south (Bergmann 2005:31).

Contemporary accounts also suggest that many of the merchants and traders seemed to be largely uninterested in taking sides in the greater political situation and were mostly concerned with the effect that the unrest had on business. Available documents indicate continued friendly business contacts between town-based traders and suppliers located within the American- and British-controlled territories (Biggs 1977:21; Cunningham 1967:29, 34; Quaife 1921; Quaife 1928: 228, 275). William Burnett, for example, was loyal to the American cause, but continued to trade through Detroit, Fort Mackinac, and Montreal, all controlled by the British (Cunningham 1967:xi). Similarly, though John Askin was a loyalist merchant in Detroit, he continued to correspond with his agents in American-controlled Vincennes (Quaife 1928:185, 226). These facts were not lost to British officials, who feared that the traders would simply begin trading with the Americans if political control of the region was transferred (Bergmann 2005:111–113).

Doing business and making a profit were key to the continuance of the fur trade, and the political troubles were treated as a nuisance. The frustration over the political situation was summed up by Burnett, who wrote in 1791 that "there is no appearance of doing anything here this year, as fear keeps the Indians from hunting. They continually imagine that the Americans are coming upon them. Add to this we have many more traders here this year than what we had last... This cursed war, that subsists between the Americans and Indians, does us more hurt in this Country than what is generally imagined" (Cunningham 1967:47–48). This was clearly an uncertain and potentially volatile situation, both for the Indian peoples of the region as well as those engaged in the fur-trade business. Despite this ambiguity, archaeological evidence supports the descriptions of Kethtippecanunk as a substantial settlement, indicating that investment by the Detroit-based merchants continued in the face of an uncertain future.

Although it is difficult to gain a detailed understanding of the availability of trade goods during this volatile time, our data suggest that there is little reason to believe that the political situation limited the traders' ability to acquire needed items for the Indian trade. One indication of this is the assemblage of gunflints found at the site. The vast majority (n = 8) was manufactured from dark-gray English Brandon flint. Brandon gunflints were not extensively manufactured until the 1790s (Kenmotsu 1990:95), indicating that the Kethtippecanunk gunflints arrived at the site shortly before its destruction. A near absence of Indian-made gunflints (n = 1) also suggests that the supplies continued without interruption.

Indian Identity within a Multiethnic Household

How can the artifacts recovered from Kethtippecanunk (particularly Block 1) shed light on the ethnic identities of the structures' inhabitants? Despite the heavy presence of European-made domestic and trade-related goods within the Block 1 excavations, a fine-grained analysis of the assemblage from this portion of the site provides evidence that this may have been a culturally mixed household. It is well known that, throughout the fur-trade period, many of the "French" traders were married to Indian women and had mixed-blood families or were of mixed blood themselves. These *métis* individuals occupied a world that was neither fully European, nor fully Indian (Peterson 1981; Sleeper-Smith 2001). John Filson, while visiting Vincennes in 1785, remarked on this fact when he noted that "numbers of the [French] inhabitants live as Savages in some respects and many are intermarried with them" (Bond 1923:328). As late as 1817, the population of the nearby village of Cattinet was similarly described as "half-breeds between French and Indian" (Flower 1882:59). Mann (2007, 2008), Sleeper-Smith (2001), Nassaney (2008), and others have noted the unique multiethnic character of fur-trade society at this time. Though the British took over much of the supply end of the Indian trade after the French and Indian War, *Canadien* traders, their American Indian spouses, and *métis* children continued to dominate commerce at the town level. Historical sources provide limited information on the names of the fur traders present at Kethtippecanunk. Of those individuals known to be associated with the town, however, all have French surnames (Quaife 1921:330–331), suggesting that a similar cultural melding was present at Kethtippecanunk as well.

As we shall see, despite the fact that many Indian women married into the fur-trade business of the Old Northwest, it is likely that the continuation of Indian identity remained important, even for those individuals who were most deeply enmeshed within the European-style market economy. The artifact assemblage from the Block 1 excavations indicates both domestic and commerce-related functions for the structures that were once present. Domestic-related artifacts include goblets, glass tumblers, forks, and European ceramics. The large rock-filled pit is obviously related to food preparation, while contents of the subfloor pit indicate that it was used for food storage.

Other artifacts indicate a commerce-related function for the structures. One of the clearest indications was the large quantity of brass tacks (n = 218). Though brass tacks were often used to decorate chests and small trunks (Noël Hume 1969: 228), they were also used by Indian individuals to decorate items such as gunstocks and war clubs (Wagner et al. 2001). It is likely that the large number of tacks in the Kethtippecanunk assemblage resulted from the destruction of a box or other container of tacks that was to be traded to the Indians. Other items possibly related to the Indian trade were numerous pieces of chest hardware, lock plates, and lock fragments. A number of silver trade items (e.g., small silver brooches and an earring fragment) were also recovered. These may have also been destined for the Indian trade, though they could also have been the personal possessions of the structures' inhabitants.

Indications of a mixed-cultural household in Block 1 include the placement of a large Indian-style tuber-roasting pit between the two probable structures. Similar pits were used by Historic period Indian peoples in northern Indiana (Cooke and Ramadhyani 1993:187). LaSalle also described their use by the 17th-century Illiniwek: "They make a hole in the earth where they put a bed of rocks reddened in the fire, then one of leaves, one of macopin [the water lily tuber], one of reddened rocks, and so on up to the top, which they cover with earth and leave their roots inside to sweat for two or three days, after which they boil them and eat them alone or with oil" (Margry 1876–1886:2). Though no tubers were found in the flotation samples taken from the roasting pit, considerable quantities of wild hyacinth root *(Camassia scilloides)* were identified from the adjacent subfloor storage pit (Bush 2007:251). These edible tubers were consumed by many Indian peoples (Medsger 1966:178), and it is presumed the tubers were being stored beneath the floorboards of the nearby structure until they could be cooked in the roasting pit.

One other possible indication of Indian identity for some of the household's inhabitants is the low relative frequency of European-made ceramics (e.g., tin-glazed earthenwares and creamware) in Block 1. Studies of late-18th- and early-19th-century assemblages suggest that even at this late date, Indian peoples shunned European-made ceramics in favor of traditional wooden vessels for food preparation and consumption (Berkson 1992; Wagner et al. 2001:131). Despite the presence of a fairly substantial, European-style structure on this spot, the Kethtippecanunk household represented in Block 1 displayed a very low density of European ceramics (only 1.52 fragments per m^2). This is compared to the assemblage from Block 2, at the northern edge of the site, in which a density of 22.71 fragments per m^2 was observed. As a test of the validity of this assertion, the frequency of other,

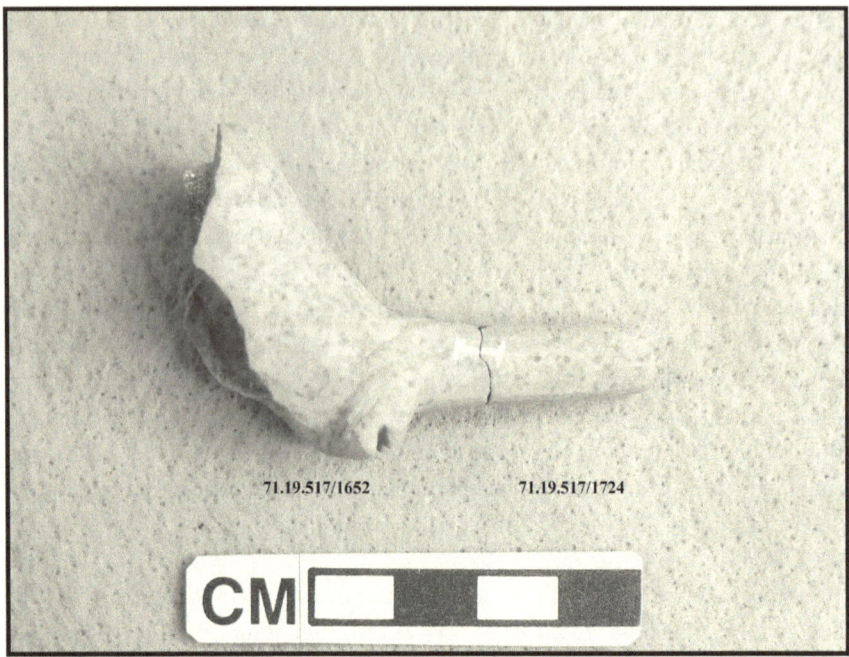

1.3. Stone pipe manufactured in the style of a white clay pipe

nonculinary-related fired-clay artifacts (i.e., white clay pipes) was compared. The frequency of white clay pipes was found to be virtually identical for the two blocks (0.33 and 0.29 fragments per m^2, respectively), suggesting that the differences in European-made ceramics are meaningful, possibly having something to do with an Indian or *métis* spouse who was most comfortable with American Indian preparation, cooking, and serving techniques.

One other possible indicator of a cross-cultural identity for the Block 1 household is the presence of a stone pipe that was manufactured in the style of a European American white clay pipe (see Figure 1.3). Though Indian peoples used European-style clay pipes for recreational smoking, they continued to manufacture and use various types of stone pipes for the ritualistic use of tobacco (Mann 2004). The Kethtippecanunk pipe then, might be conceived as mixture of European and Indian smoking cultures (Trubowitz 1992b), possibly by someone who was familiar with both traditions. Though rare, stone imitations of European-style pipes have been found at both Indian and European sites in the immediate area, including the Zachariah Cicott trading post (Mann 2004:174) and the Wea village, a purely Indian habitation site (Trubowitz 1992b:104).

Finally, it is likely that one of the male residents of the structure held a more European cultural identity. This assertion is supported by the presence of two Masonic artifacts. Masonry was an institution that was fully within the European cultural sphere, and it is unlikely that any persons with an Indian cultural identity were members. The first of the two artifacts is a "TD" pipe bowl with a Masonic compass, while the second is a fob seal with a coat of arms from the Premier Grand Lodge of England. Of interest is the fact that local lodges associated with the overarching Premier Grand Lodge were mostly those that supported the British cause during the Revolutionary War (Bullock 1996). Considering the pro-British position of the traders and Indian peoples of the Wabash, the association of this artifact with Kethtippecanunk is not surprising. Since both French and British Freemasons were resident in Detroit prior to 1764, the presence of Masonic artifacts adds little to our ability to answer the question of whether or not this particular trader was of British or French background (Grand Lodge of Free and Accepted Masons of the State of Michigan 2007). Overall, the assemblage from Block 1 provides a mixed bag of evidence, something to be expected in a household with a cultural identity that was not wholly European or Indian.

Conclusion

Many Indian towns involved in the fur trade were relatively affluent (Sleeper-Smith 2001:5), and both the documentary and archaeological evidence indicate that the residents of Kethtippecanunk had reaped the benefits of participation in this enterprise. At a site like this one, the activities of Indian peoples were deeply intertwined with those of the fur traders, and the economic aims of the two groups have to be examined together to gain a full understanding of the assemblage. What is abundantly clear, however, is that participation in the trade for European goods (whether as an individual trading furs for desired items or as the spouse of a fur trader) did not fundamentally transform Indian peoples and make them "less Indian" (Ehrhardt 2005:21; Trubowitz 1992b). By the same token, the transformation/integration of ethnically French traders via contact with Indian peoples was a means to gain access to Indian kin networks, build alliances, and reduce their "foreignness" to American Indians, rather than the sad degeneration of previously "civilized" peoples (White 1991:59, 69). Both the French and American Indians participating in the fur-trade economy were active decision makers who chose whether to use, modify, or reject items from the other's culture. The mutual influence they exerted upon one another in the realms of clothing, foodways, adornment, and technology brings to light the means through which material goods can act within social, symbolic, and economic contexts.

Acknowledgments

I would like to thank the co-director of the excavations, Bob McCullough, for his help in the planning, logistics, execution, and interpretation during the 2005 and 2006 field seasons at Kethtippecanunk. Dot McCullough, Rick Jones, Josh Wells, and Craig Arnold were coauthors on one or both of the site reports for the two field seasons and aspects of their work are also incorporated into this chapter. The staff at Prophetstown State Park was very accommodating and sacrificed a portion of their prairie restoration for the sake of archaeology. Finally, Del Bartlett and the Tippecanoe County Historical Association have been supportive of our work at the site and also deserve thanks. Funding for the 2005 field season at Kethtippecanunk was provided by an American Battlefield Protection Program grant (GA-2255-04-004), while the 2006 investigations were supported by a U.S. Department of the Interior, National Park Service Historic Preservation Grant, administered by the Indiana Department of Natural Resources, Division of Historic Preservation and Archaeology.

2 / "Remarkable Elasticity of Character"
Colonial Discourse, the Market Economy, and Catawba Itinerancy, 1770–1820

Mark R. Plane

Introduction

Understanding colonies and colonialism has become a major focus of archaeological research. Efforts to create a unifying theory of colonialism have justifiably been declared "reductive ventures" that reify a highly variable, transhistorical phenomenon (Dietler 2007:220). Nevertheless, Gil Stein (2005:7) notes the development of a new paradigm in studies of colonialism and other forms of interregional interaction. Within this paradigm, archaeological research concentrating on agency, practice, and social identity has been particularly important.

Postcolonial studies stress the importance of discourse in shaping colonial institutions and identities (see, e.g., Bhabha 1994; McClintock 1995; Said 1978, 1993). Racial discourses shaped the understanding of European colonists, constraining how settlers approached and reacted to colonized people (Bhabha 1994; Said 1978, 1993). These discourses, widely circulated in a variety of cultural venues, served to naturalize and legitimize domination of non-Europeans (Said 1993; van Dommelen 2005). Within both European and colonial contexts, these discourses also played an important role in constructing racial or ethnic identities, as Europeans, colonized peoples, and other subaltern groups engaged in dialectical processes of defining themselves in opposition to one another (Bhabha 1994; Fanon 1968; Raibmon 2005:3, 10–14; Said 1978, 1993).

Postcolonial theorists such as Franz Fanon (1968) have argued that colonial societies were often highly influential in defining the identities of colonized people. Nonetheless, even as colonialism limited social and economic opportunities for colonized peoples, the latter were able to manipulate colonial institutions to their advantage. For example, through strategic mimicry of Western practices and discourses, colonial subjects pursued personal and nationalist agendas (Bhabha 1994; McClintock 1995). Colonized people also manipulated racial discourses by "playing native" for Europeans in the pursuit of economic, cultural, and political gain (see, e.g., Moses 1996; Phillips 1995, 1998; Raibmon 2005).

In this chapter, I explore the relationship between colonialism, European racial discourses, and indigenous practice and identity through research on Catawba Indians in late-18th- and early-19th-century Piedmont South Carolina (ca. 1770–1820). Utilizing both archaeological and documentary evidence, I focus on how the Catawba Nation responded to population decline and an increasing European presence. This time period marks the end of the Catawbas' dominant role in colonial-era trade and warfare. With the passing of the frontier, and a rapid influx of white settlers into Catawba territory, this period also marks the beginning of new economic strategies within Catawba society, including leasing reservation land to settlers, Catawba men working as slave catchers for plantation owners, and Catawba women engaging in an itinerant trade in handmade pottery.

In this study, I present archaeological and documentary perspectives on Catawba itinerancy. I examine the likely origin and socioeconomic function of the Catawba pottery trade and how racial discourses shaped Europeans' perceptions of the Catawba, both on their reservation and on the road. Finally, I explore how the Catawba may have strategically manipulated racial discourses, and the role that the pottery trade and racial discourses may have played in the formation of Catawba identity.

Indians in European Discourse

Discourses act as filters in the interpretation of human experience, as the terms and procedures that regulate how and what people communicate, and serve to support networks of power relations (Foucault 1972; Lincoln 1989). European racial discourses were often very rigid, typically involving limited sets of stereotypes tailored to suit particular contexts (Bhabha 1994). Discourses on the Indian invariably served political and economic purposes. A widespread European racial discourse in the late 18th and early 19th century pronounced the incompatibility of savage and civilized races. As colonialism transformed indigenous societies, the contrast between "wild, uncivilized savages" and so-called degenerate Indians became an important facet of racial discourse (Berkhofer 1978:36–38; Bieder 1986; Young 1995).

Wild savages were figured as nomadic warriors and hunters, creatures of the forest living in a state of nature. Depending on the observer's politics and motivations, wild Indians might be seen as good or bad. Good Indians were depicted as noble, modest, calm, courageous in combat, and dignified in bearing. They lived wholesome and healthy lives, characterized by love of family, independence, rugged simplicity, and innocence (Berkhofer 1978:27–28; Bieder 1986:5; Deloria 1998:2–5; Raibmon 2005:6–8). On the other hand, bad Indians were described as vain, promiscuous, bloodthirsty, cruel, cowardly, treacherous, and indolent; their lifestyles were described in terms of filthy surroundings, loathsome habits, and nauseating foodways (Berkhofer 1978:27–28; Bieder 1986:5; Deloria 1998:2–5; Raibmon 2005:6–8).

These images of the wild Indian were set in opposition to another stereotype, that of the "degenerate," or "degraded," reservation Indian. Unable or unwilling to receive the benefits of assimilation into white society, degenerate Indians lived in the worst of both worlds. Shunned by whites—and self-respecting wild Indians as well—degenerate Indians retained the most loathsome aspects of savagery, while readily adopting white vices. Degenerate Indians were portrayed as drunken, idle, filthy, dependent, disorderly, servile, and desperately impoverished (Berkhofer 1978:29–30).

By the late 18th century the idea of the vanishing race became part of white discourse on Indians. With extinction, marginalization, and removal, the vanishing Indian was not necessarily viewed as an imminent threat to life, morals, and commerce. Indeed, for many whites, as Indian societies dwindled and disappeared, they became exotic curiosities, and romantic images of the ancient or colonial past readily replaced those that inspired sentiments of fear and loathing (Berkhofer 1978:29; Deloria 1998:64).

Indians were quick to capitalize on this discursive shift. For example, in her research on cultural "authenticity" among American Indians in the late 19th century on the Northwest coast, Paige Raibmon (2005:3, 10–14) describes how indigenous groups both incorporated and manipulated colonialist discourse on Indians, in effect "playing Indian" for economic, cultural, and political gains. Working seasonally as pickers for hop farmers, thousands of aboriginal people from Washington, British Columbia, and Alaska converged on Washington hop fields each August. According to a contemporary narrator (Lindsay 1899:534–539), the Indians "conjured up confused visions . . . of a Prehistoric World and a Vanished Race." The spectacle of Indian pickers became the basis of a major tourist industry, as white tourists flocked to rural towns to view "authentic" Indians in the hop fields and at their encampments (Raibmon 2005:198–199).

The seasonal, migratory nature of agricultural work fit neatly into colonialist discourse on nomadic savages; moreover, whites tended to view the temporary presence of Indians as a romantic show rather than a threat (Raibmon 2005:167–168). Fully aware of white stereotypes of savages, Indians readily seized upon economic opportunities created by tourism. In addition to farmwork, Indian men worked as hunting and fishing guides for tourists, while women sold handmade baskets, blankets, and carvings. Indians also frequently posed for photographs and even staged paid-admission ritual dance performances (Raibmon 2005:90–93).

Despite the commercialization of Indian identity by tourists and Indians, Raibmon (2005:12) emphasizes the ways in which indigenous people twisted colonial concepts such as "savagery" and "authenticity" to their own ends. Thus, the performance of Indian identity in the marketplace cannot be seen as a mere commercial ploy, but rather, a process of "crafting tradition and continuity through repeated and contested use" of cultural forms (Raibmon 2005:12). In order to articulate cultural difference, ethnic and racial outsiders may restage and reinscribe the past (Bhabha 1994:3), using available forms and within existing cultural contexts.

Historical Roots of Catawba Itinerancy: Colonialism and Indian Identity within a Shatter Zone

Extensive mobility characterized American Indian life in the eastern woodlands of North America by the early 18th century. Ironically, the nomadism that Europeans believed was as an essential characteristic of the Indian race was in many ways a product of colonialism. The eastern woodlands had become a "shatter zone," due to instability created by the introduction of the capitalist market system through the Indian slave trade in the 17th century. Indian societies were engaged in widespread and intensive warfare and slaving, with rival Indian groups pitted against one another by competing colonial interests. Combined with population losses from disease epidemics, the result was a zone of tremendous political chaos, population dislocation, and sociocultural transformation (Ethridge 2006; Heath 2004).

With the English settlement of Charles Town in 1670, the Catawbas' location on a critical trading path ensured them an important role in the competition between colonial powers (Fitts 2006; Heath 2004; Moore 2002). By the early 18th century, the Catawba had become a military power and the host community of a confederation of Piedmont tribes (Davis and Riggs 2004; Fitts 2006; Heath 2004; Merrell 1989).

Catawba warriors acted as "ethnic soldiers," buffering colonial South Carolina from the French and their Indian allies (Heath 2004). Empires use ethnic soldiers as auxiliary combat troops and internal police to control subversive or enslaved populations (Ferguson and Whitehead 1999). As ethnic soldiers, the Catawba earned a reputation as fierce and skillful warriors, which in turn earned them status as a favored trading partner with colonial South Carolina (Heath 2004).

Archaeological and documentary evidence clearly demonstrate the Catawbas' growing dependence upon British trade for their everyday needs (see, e.g., Brown 1966; Davis and Riggs 2004; Fitts 2006; Heath 2004; Merrell 1989). Documentary evidence also demonstrates British influence over Catawba identity, as British colonists, Catawba warriors, and apparently other Indians all embraced the Catawbas' reputation for martial prowess (Heath 2004; Merrell 1989). Thus, Edmond Atkin, a Carolina trader and British superintendent of Indian Affairs emphatically stated that "in war they are inferior [to] no Indians whatever . . . Such is the Honour in Indian Estimation to be acquired by Killing any of them, that Indians as far as the [Great] Lakes go in quest of them" (Jacobs 1967:47). In 1756, the Catawba leader King Hagler boasted to a South Carolina governor, "We are a small Nation but our Name is high, and if we go to the War with the White People against the enemy we shall drive them so far as that we shall raise many Children without any Danger or Molestation" (McDowell 1969:107–108).

Warfare took a heavy toll on the Catawba confederacy and Catawbas recruited shatter zone refugees to staunch population losses (Merrell 1989:101–106). As a result of recruiting efforts, by 1743 over twenty different languages were spoken in Catawba settlements, with some tribal groups living in distinct towns (Adair 1930).

Augmented by refugees, the Catawba Nation for a time maintained dominance among Piedmont tribes; however, between 1700 and 1759, incessant warfare, disease, and defection had reduced the Catawba confederacy from an estimated population of six to eight thousand individuals to little more than one thousand (McReynolds 2004:44–45). In 1759, a smallpox epidemic decimated what remained of the Catawba and their allies, killing perhaps 50–60 percent of the confederacy's population (Brown 1966:180–181; Merrell 1989:194–195). The survivors abandoned their towns and regrouped, staying for several months near the settlement of Pine Tree Hill, at present-day Camden, South Carolina.

In 1761, the survivors returned to Catawba territory and condensed six towns into just two. By 1781, there was but one Catawba settlement, known as Old Town. At this point, the distinct identities of the different tribal groups were apparently erased, leaving what Indians and colonists referred to as simply "the Catawba" (Davis and Riggs 2004).

After the 1759 epidemic, the Catawbas' military and political influence waned. Although the Catawba no longer possessed sufficient warriors to play an important military role, their loyalty to South Carolina and reputation as fierce savages opened up another economic and political opportunity: serving as runaway-slave catchers. In 1765, South Carolina lieutenant governor William Bull called upon Catawba warriors to capture escaped slaves hiding in the swamps outside Charles Town, asserting that, "Indians strike terrour [sic] into the Negroes," and were "more sagacious in tracking" than colonists (Merrell 1989:144). In 1775–76, Catawba warriors, having cast their lot with the American Revolutionaries, were called upon to hunt both runaway slaves and Tories in the lowcountry (Merrell 1989:207, 216). Catawba warriors also joined a state militia in attacking an escaped slave camp on the Savannah River in 1787 (Bentley 1991).

These policing ventures brought large parties of Catawbas to the South Carolina lowcountry for extended periods of time (Merrell 1989:207, 216); however, unlike the frontier proxy wars in which they previously fought, Catawba warriors pursued runaway slaves near the very center of colonial power. Throughout much of the colonial era, Catawba diplomatic missions often visited colonial officials in Charleston and at their lowcountry plantation homes (Brown 1966; Merrell 1989). Indeed, colonial records reveal that between 1720 and 1760, such diplomatic visits increased not only in frequency, but also in terms of the size of Catawba parties, which came to include not only headmen and warriors, but women and children as well (Brown 1966:221–222; Merrell 1989:145–146). Visits to colonial officials were opportunities to obtain valuable intelligence and trade goods and, more important, to remain on the political map by reminding influential allies of the Catawbas' continued loyalty and usefulness.

The Catawba appear to have been engaged in slave catching on a limited basis; however, Charles Hudson (1970:58) notes that the myth of Indian savagery was an effective tool that planters used to intimidate slaves, even after the Catawba were no longer a military force to be reckoned with. At a time when the passing of the frontier and the Catawbas' declining population cast considerable doubt on their continued usefulness, such opportunities would have been critical to maintaining their position in South Carolina society. Embracing the roles they played for European settlers became a matter of survival. Performing these roles was not only a matter of what Catawbas did for Europeans, but also, as the statements of both Catawbas and colonists reveal, how Europeans *perceived* what Catawbas did. This has important implications for the development of the Catawbas' pottery trade, an activity that, like slave catching, involved traveling to the center of colonial power, and undoubtedly hinged upon images of the Indian that were understood by Indians and Europeans alike.

The Catawba and Backcountry Settlers

During the height of the slave and deerskin trades in the early 18th century, backcountry traders and lowcountry government officials were the Catawbas' most significant European contacts. By the mid 18th century, the slave trade was over and the Piedmont deerskin trade was winding down. As settlers invaded Catawba territory, relationships with the settlers themselves became of greater importance (Brown 1966:297; Merrell 1989:209–212).

Pressured by settler encroachment, in 1760 the Catawba relinquished claims to most of their land in exchange for legal title to a 15-square-mile reservation. Some time after the creation of this reservation in 1763, white farmers began to rent land from the Catawba (Merrell 1989:198–200). At the time of the Revolutionary

War, the Catawba had rented large tracts on the reservation to at least three settler families (Merrell 1989:198–200). By 1791, some three hundred settlers leased land on the reservation. By the early 19th century, all but several hundred of the 144,000-acre Catawba reservation had been rented to settlers (Brown 1966:297; Merrell 1989:209–210).

For many tenants, lease arrangements provided access to land they could not otherwise afford. For the Catawba, this system not only provided income, but also gave settlers a stake in the continued existence of the Catawba Nation. Whereas neither squatters nor the South Carolina government had much concern for the Catawba Nation's legal title, tenants became the Catawbas' "night watchmen," each guarding their respective tract of land against encroachment by squatters while Catawbas were away chasing slaves and selling pottery.

Documentary evidence suggests that tenants often cheated their Catawba landlords (Brown 1966:297; Merrell 1989:230–237; Pettus 2005:39–44). Lease arrangements nonetheless created a détente between settlers and the Catawba, and provided Catawba families with cash, food, and goods for perhaps 70 years. More important, the lease system served to perpetuate the idea of the Catawba Nation, despite its rapidly declining numbers—between 1759 and 1820, the Catawba population fell from approximately one thousand to perhaps three hundred individuals (McReynolds 2004).

The lease system enabled the Catawba to maintain landownership until 1840. At that time, the South Carolina legislature, urged by Catawba tenants who were concerned that land speculators were attempting to gain control of the reservation, convinced the Catawba to cede their lands in exchange for large cash payments and a tract of land to be purchased by the state. The reservation was dissolved and Catawbas resettled among the Cherokee in North Carolina. Although the promises made by the state were not honored, some time around 1850 many of the Catawba returned to South Carolina, when they were given 630 acres of land on their original reservation (Hudson 1970:64–65; Merrell 1989:257).

Overview of Colonoware and the Catawba Pottery Trade

The term *colonoware* refers to unglazed, low-fired earthenware of demonstrably European influence (Ferguson 1992). Colonowares have been recovered on sites in Florida, Georgia, North and South Carolina, and Virginia (Ferguson 1992). These wares are particularly common in late-18th- and early-19th-century archaeological contexts in South Carolina (Ferguson 1992; Riggs et al. 2006). South Carolina colonowares attributed by archaeologists to Catawba potters have generally been from late-18th- and early-19th-century lowcountry contexts (Ferguson 1989; Garrow and Wheaton 1989). Colonowares from 17th through mid-18th-century lowcountry contexts have generally been attributed to coastal Indian tribes, settlement Indians, and enslaved Indians and Africans (Ferguson 1992:18–22; Garrow and Wheaton 1989).

While colonowares are too varied and widespread to be attributable to any single source, there is no doubt that Catawbas were engaged in manufacturing and trading colonowares from the 1770s up to the present day, producing in turn utilitarian wares, tourist items, and more recently, art pottery for the Indian arts and crafts market (Blumer 2004; Fewkes 1944; Harrington 1908; Riggs et al. 2006).

As demonstrated by archaeological and documentary evidence, Catawba potters served market demands for inexpensive utilitarian pottery through an itinerant trade that was conducted for some 50 years across large portions of South Carolina (Baker 1972, 1976; Ferguson 1989; Merrell 1989; Riggs et al. 2006). Catawba pottery has been recovered from plantation sites across several counties in lowcountry South Carolina (Ferguson 1989; Garrow and Wheaton 1989; Wheaton et al. 1983); it has also been recovered on backcountry sites, including historic Camden (Lewis 1976) and the William R. Davie plantation, where it was found at both the main house and slave cabin sites (Riggs et al. 2006:79). European visitors to the Catawba Nation described Catawba women making and selling pottery for trade in the 1770s, 1780s, and again in 1815 (Jones 1815; Smyth 1784). Nineteenth-century observers remarked on Catawba women trading pottery locally (Scaife 1930), in the vicinity of Columbia (Scott 1884), and while traveling from the upcountry to Charleston (Gregory 1925).

The link between documentary accounts and colonowares excavated in a variety of lowcountry and backcountry contexts has been secured by analyses of domestic contexts excavated by the UNC Research Laboratories of Archaeology at the Catawba town sites of Nassaw Town (inhabited ca. 1750–59), Old Town (inhabited ca. 1770–80) and New Town (inhabited ca. 1781–1820). While ceramics recovered from Nassaw Town have not yet been fully analyzed, preliminary analysis suggests that Catawbas were not manufacturing colonoware forms at that time. Nassaw ceramic assemblages are composed primarily of hemispheric and carinated bowls, along with restricted neck jars and bottles; unlike flat-bottomed colonoware vessels, pots at Nassaw Town had rounded bottoms. Along with some plain, burnished vessels, a wide variety of decorative techniques are represented, including cord marking, simple and complicated stamping, fine and bold incising, and punctation. The complete absence of colonoware forms at Nassaw suggests that the Catawbas' itinerant trade in the lowcountry began after the 1759 smallpox epidemic.

In contrast, an abundance of colonowares has been recovered from Old Town and New Town. Old and New Town Catawba wares are primarily replicas of imported English vessel forms, including foot-ringed teacups and bowls, porringers, patty pans, chamber pots, milk pans, and soup plates (see Figure 2.1).

"Remarkable Elasticity of Character" 41

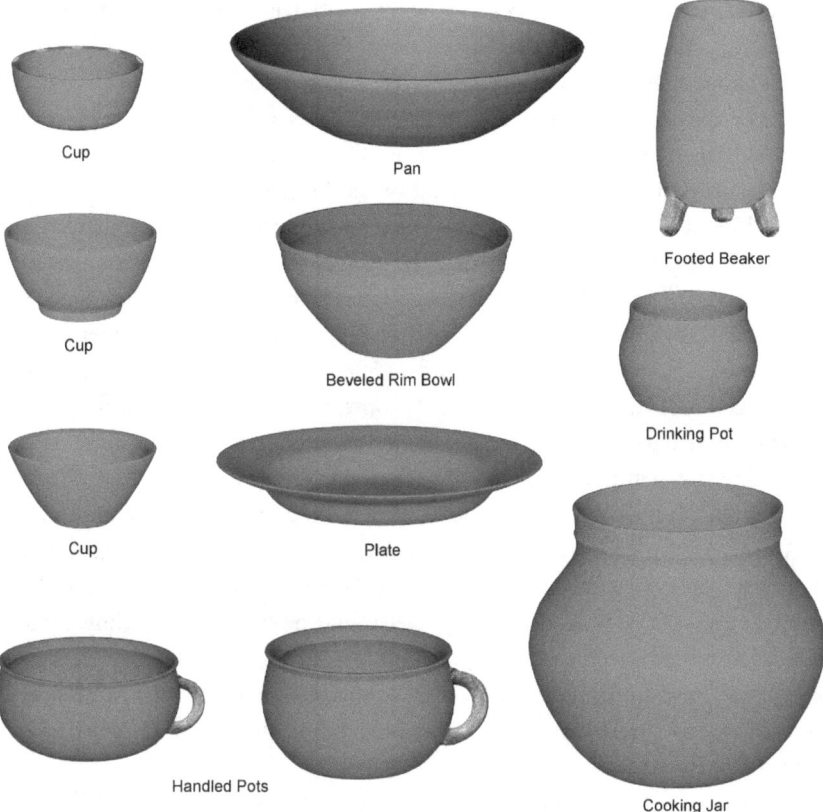

2.1. Digital reconstructions of common Catawba vessel forms

All vessel forms at Old Town and New Town were flat bottomed—even restricted-neck cooking pots, vessels otherwise aboriginal in form. Many of these wares were highly burnished and smother-fired to a jet-black color (usually on the interior surface), as described by 19th- and 20th-century observers (Fewkes 1944; Harrington 1908; Jones 1815). Much like imported English wares, some colonoware vessels were painted along the rims and shoulders. When painted, Old Town vessels were decorated with either red slip or lines executed in black pigment. At New Town, Catawba potters used orange or silver-blue pigmented sealing wax, decorative treatments described by the 19th-century author William Gilmore Simms (2003a). Aside from burnishing, none of the decorative techniques seen at Nassaw Town occur in Old and New Town assemblages (although a single New Town vessel had burnishing over shallow incising). The demands of the marketplace appear to have superseded any other concerns in pottery manufacture and usage among Catawbas in these communities.

The quality of Catawba wares and the substantial quantities of a wide variety of imported English tablewares recovered from Old and New Town Catawba cabin sites demonstrate that Catawba potters were highly informed producers and consumers of ceramics. Indeed, well-executed teawares and serving wares recovered from Old Town demonstrate that Catawba potters possessed considerable knowledge of European tablewares by the time of the American Revolution.

The lack of colonowares at Nassaw Town and abundance and sophistication of these wares at Old Town suggest that the pottery trade developed soon after the abandonment of Catawba settlements in 1759. The trade may have developed during the Catawbas' encampment at Pine Tree Hill in 1760 or during extended lowcountry slave catching forays in the mid-1760s. The occurrence of colonowares in early- and mid-18th-century lowcountry contexts and the Catawbas' frequent absorption of refugees suggests the possibility that they adopted personnel already engaged in the manufacture and trade of colonowares; such individuals may have been settlement Indians living in the vicinity of Pine Tree Hill or Charleston.

A single cabin site has been excavated at Catawba Old Town. A large cellar pit at this site yielded a wide variety of materials, including nearly two thousand glass beads; several coins, brass and silver jewelry, and ornaments, including a pair of cuff links with glass insets; needles, pins, and scissors; a mirror; knives; various glassware fragments; gunflints and lead shot; numerous fragments of Catawba-made tobacco pipes; a small quantity of kaolin pipe fragments; and nearly one thousand Catawba potsherds.

Analysis of Catawba pottery recovered from the cabin site at Old Town has yielded an estimated minimum of 37 vessels. The assemblage of Catawba-made pottery consists entirely of European-influenced vessel forms, including foot-ringed bowls and tea bowls, patty pans, polygonal soup plates (see Figure 2.2), and milk pans. Many individual serving wares were made using clay that fired to a pale gray, perhaps emulating the light-colored bodies of creamwares and early pearlwares. Some vessels were decorated with swag-and-dot designs executed in a black pigment; a few were decorated with a red slip. This site also yielded a small collection of sherds from imported English ceramics, representing at least six vessels, including a large hand-painted enamel porcelain punch bowl, three teacups, and two saucers.

Five cabin sites at Catawba New Town have been excavated; ceramic assemblages from two cabin sites have been thoroughly analyzed. Excavation at these two cabin sites yielded a tremendous quantity of artifacts, including some three hundred glass beads; brass kettle and iron Dutch oven fragments; numerous pieces of brass and silver jewelry and ornaments; brass buckles; brass and silver buttons; scissors, needles, pins, and thimbles; spoons, knives, and forks; several padlocks; nearly a dozen mouth harps; a variety of tools, gun parts, flints, and lead shot; several snaffle bits and other pieces of horse tack and wagon hardware.

The frequent appearance of horse tack and wagon hardware on Catawba cabin

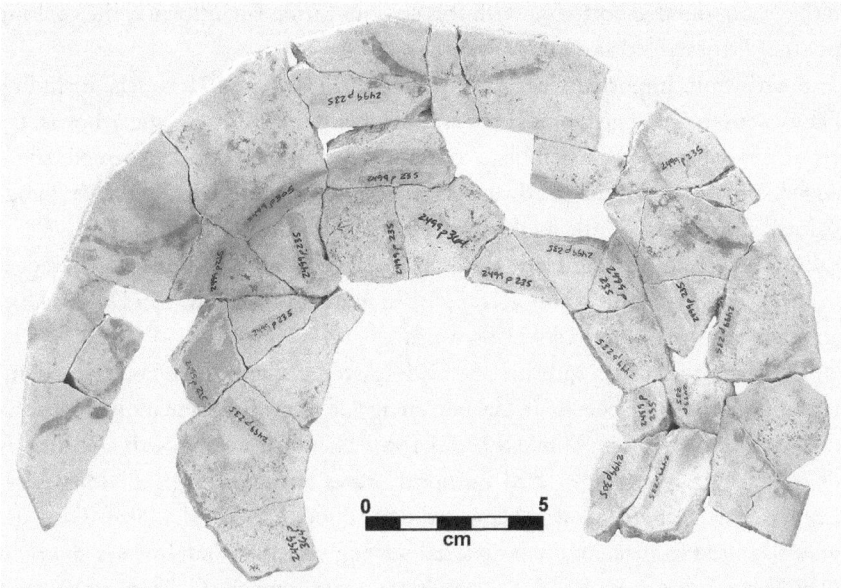

2.2. Polygonal soup plate with edge decoration

sites has significant implications for Catawba itinerancy. In comparative research on Gypsy itinerants, the most successful and wide-ranging groups owned both means of transportation, such as horses and wagons, and houses where they settled during winter months (Barnes 1975:251).

Ceramic assemblages from the two New Town cabins include some two hundred fragments of Catawba-made tobacco pipes, three kaolin pipe fragments, nearly two thousand sherds from imported European serving wares, and nearly 20 thousand Catawba potsherds. In addition to the Catawba pottery, some two dozen wear-faceted burnishing stones used in pottery making were recovered, suggesting a level of production that could best be described as craft specialization.

The Catawba pottery recovered from these two New Town cabin sites represents a minimum of 99 vessels. The assemblages of Catawba-made pottery consist of a variety of European-influenced vessel forms, including teacups, foot-ringed bowls, porringers, chamber pots, soup plates, milk pans, and even substantial portions of a Moravian-style footed coffee pot. A small percentage of New Town vessels was painted with orange or silver-blue colored sealing wax. On painted vessels, rim stripes were the most common decoration; however, potters also applied decorations resembling floral designs found on imported pearlwares.

These assemblages also include sherds from restricted-neck cooking pots (see Figure 2.1). In terms of the rim, neck, and body, the latter vessels are similar to pots recovered at Nassaw Town; however, the versions found at New Town have flat rather than rounded bottoms. With this obvious European influence, the cooking pot may be described as a colonoware vessel.

Sherds from imported English wares represent at least 121 vessels, including plates, soup plates, cups, mugs, bowls, chamber pots, creamers, sugar bowls, tea cups, and saucers. The assemblage contains creamwares, transfer-printed, shell-edged, and hand-painted pearlwares, annular wares, stonewares, and even hand-painted porcelains. While analyses of ceramics from the remaining New Town cabin sites are not yet complete, the assemblages appear very similar in character. Catawba women were not only accomplished potters, but also avid and knowledgeable consumers of imported serving wares.

One factor that distinguishes the Old Town and New Town ceramic assemblages is a dramatic decrease in the percentage of Catawba-made individual serving wares at New Town. While the Old Town assemblage consists almost entirely of colonoware vessels, imported European wares largely fill the individual serving vessel niche at New Town (Plane and Ladu 2006; Riggs et al. 2006). The pale-gray clay used to make many individual serving vessels at Old Town is absent at New Town; moreover, foot-ringed bowls constitute a much smaller percentage of colonowares. Catawba-made vessels at New Town are primarily large milk pans, chamber pots, and cooking pots, although a substantial percentage of soup plates are still present (Plane and Ladu 2006).

Tobacco pipes recovered from Catawba town sites provide an interesting contrast to serving wares. Imported kaolin tobacco pipes—abundant on the 1750s Nassaw Town site, and infrequent at Old Town—had all but completely disappeared at Catawba New Town (see Figure 2.3). This runs completely counter to the historical trend of increasing popularity for imported kaolin pipes, and near disappearance of Indian-made pipes, on both settler *and* Indian sites in the region during this time period (Bollwerk 2007).

Catawba pipes underwent a curious transformation between the mid 18th and early 19th centuries. Catawba-made pipes recovered from both Nassaw and Old Town are primarily Calumet style, with relatively long stems and large bowls; all appear to be handmade, most of clay, but some from Nassau Town are carved from stone; decoration is minimal or absent. New Town pipes are mold made, and instead of forms in which the bowl is permanently attached to a long stem, the pipes consist of relatively smaller clay bowls with very short stems to which reeds were attached (Riggs et al. 2006). In addition, New Town pipes were typically decorated with incisions and punctuations; some were also painted with the same bright-orange-colored sealing wax used to decorate ceramic vessels.

This shift in pipe production evident at New Town does not coincide with the shift to colonoware production, as the earlier Old Town assemblage is already composed entirely of colonoware forms. Instead it occurs after the Catawba are believed to have stayed for a time with the Pamunkey Indians in Virginia. Having

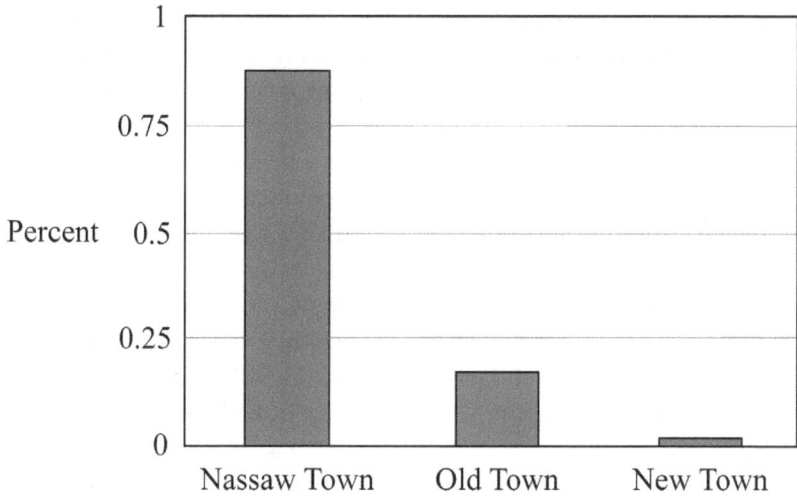
2.3. Percentages of kaolin pipe fragments recovered at Catawba town sites

sided with the Revolutionaries, the Catawba were forced to flee the British army in 1780; they stayed in Virginia for nearly a year (Merrell 1989:216 n. 78). Post-Revolutionary Catawba pipes are remarkably similar in form and plastic decoration to pipes made by Pamunkeys for market trade (Bollwerk 2007).

In terms of Catawba identity, ceramics recovered from Catawba town sites seem to present some contradictions. Catawba women continued to produce pottery, but abandoned traditional forms and decorations, as commodities for market trade. From the composition of the New Town assemblages, it would appear that food and drink were typically prepared and set out in Catawba pottery, but consumed from imported English vessels; these trends could be interpreted as evidence of acculturation. Imported kaolin pipes fell out of fashion among Catawbas, who chose instead to use pipes of their own manufacture; moreover, Catawbas did continue to make and use their own handmade pottery, trends that could be interpreted as a form of resistance. Are European goods in Catawba contexts evidence of acculturation? Were Catawba-made pots and pipes markers of Indian identity and symbols of tradition and resistance, or mere commodities? The answer, most likely, is more complicated than dichotomies such as Western versus traditional or acculturation versus resistance.

Rather than an index of acculturation, I would argue that imported serving wares were markers of a distinctive Catawba identity, perhaps representing a Catawba potter's knowledge of the pottery market and her success in the itinerant trade. However, as these markers were displayed and used in relatively private, domestic contexts, they were presumably intended for the benefit of other Catawbas, rather than outside observers. Given the poly-ethnic makeup of Catawba society, imported and Catawba-made ceramics may both have played an important role in Catawba ethnogenesis. Perhaps in addition to being an economic strategy, making, selling, and buying pottery were means through which women from diverse tribal backgrounds participated in the formation of a common Catawba identity.

As for pipes, while imported serving wares were used in relatively private, domestic contexts, tobacco pipes would have been used in both private and public settings. It is interesting to consider that from a marketing perspective, using European dishes in private would have been invisible to the Catawbas' white customers. However, using European pipes in public would have been visible and counterproductive in terms of marketing both Catawba pottery and the Catawba Nation. In this sense, the overwhelming predominance of Catawba-made pipes at Old Town and New Town may represent the development of both an ethnic marker and a veritable market "brand."

The Catawbas' pottery trade represents a perfect synthesis of the economic and political potentials of the marketing of Indian identity. As was the case in ethnic soldiering and land leasing, the itinerant pottery trade was likely to have addressed both political and economic needs. Traveling to sell pottery generated income and provided the Catawba with access to influential South Carolinians. Visits to plantations by Catawba potters and their families undoubtedly served as opportunities to remind powerful people of the Catawbas' continued loyalty. Through their itinerant lifestyle, Catawba families no doubt tapped into well-known colonial discourses on nomadic wild savages, presenting planters with a striking image of the Catawba Nation as a vital entity that continued to play a useful role in South Carolina society.

Discourse in Documentary Accounts of Life on the Catawba Reservation

Although only a handful of European accounts of life on the Catawba reservation survive, all are quite grim in their overall assessment of Catawba life. The authors of these accounts are obviously familiar with discourses on Indian savagery, degeneration, and extinction.

Typical of these accounts is that of John Ferdinand Smyth, published in 1784. Smyth was a British soldier who traveled extensively in the North American colonies, visiting the Catawba in the early 1770s. In his account, Smyth (1784:118–125) relied heavily on images of Indian degeneration, emphasizing the Catawbas' poverty and misery and the loss of their savage nature.

Smyth (1784:119) described the Catawba as "dwindled away almost to nothing ... and such they are, as would excite the derision and contempt of the more western savages, for these are in a kind of state of civilization." Noting that "the Catawbas afford a melancholy example ... of the ruin and fatality brought on any Indian nation, by the intemperance and vicinity of the settlements of the whites . . . ," Smyth concluded that the Catawbas were "indeed a poor, inoffensive, insignificant people, enveloped in filth and nastiness of person . . . who seem indeed, in a great measure, to have lost that martial independent spirit, for which that whole race of mankind have been ever distinguished and to be sinking fast into degeneracy and a state of servility and dependence, inferior even to the most indigent of the whites" (119–124).

Another interesting account is contained in a letter penned by David Hutchison, a Scots-Irish tenant of the Catawbas who lived on the reservation from the 1780s until his death in 1845. Referring to the time period between the Revolutionary War and the abandonment of New Town in the 1820s, Hutchison wrote, "By the time the Indians ceased spending so much of their time down the country, the Leaseholders had a reasonable quantity of Land cleared . . . When the Indians came home they had given up all idea of farming. The women had formerly attended to this department, but they came home as lazy, indolent, and intemperate as the men." Hutchison focused on familiar themes of Indian degeneracy: drunkenness and indolence, writing that Catawbas "spent their time in traveling about collecting their rents and lying about still-houses and grog shops" (Brown 1966:291–292).

Hutchison's claim that the Catawba women gave up "all idea of farming" after the Revolution is perhaps an exaggeration, but it is nevertheless buttressed by both archaeological and documentary evidence. At Nassaw Town, substantial quantities of charred cobs were recovered from a variety of contexts, including numerous smudge pits—small, shallow, circular features presumably used in pottery production (interestingly, Calvin Jones and subsequent observers of Catawba pottery production describe Catawba women smudging pots using bark rather than corncobs; Fewkes 1944; Harrington 1908; Jones 1815). At Old Town, numerous corncobs were recovered from subsurface pit features. Relatively speaking, extraordinarily little maize has been recovered from any of the cabin sites excavated at New Town. In his account of the Catawba from 1791, the Reverend Thomas Coke wrote: "They possess a quantity of land, fifteen miles square . . . A very small part of this land they cultivate themselves: a much larger part they let out in long leases to the white people" (Brown 1966:288).

If indeed the Catawba were no longer, or only minimally, engaged in agriculture, they must have relied instead upon food they received through purchase, barter, and foraging. In his visit to New Town, Calvin Jones (1815) succinctly described the Catawbas' economy: "Men gone hunting and fishing. Women making pans—Clay from the river—shape them with their hands and burn them with bark which makes the exposed side a glossy black. A pitcher a quarter of a dollar. Sell pans frequently for the full [measure] of meal. Saw some sitting on their beds and making pans." Obtaining food from commercial activity rather than primary production is typical for itinerant groups (Rao 1987). Leasing reservation land and making pottery were strategic choices made by Catawbas in the allocation of resources and time; these choices precluded or greatly limited other economic possibilities.

In general, the accounts present a gloomy portrait of Catawba life. While the Catawbas undoubtedly suffered hardships, observers' accounts of Catawba life contradict themselves and one another; moreover, in certain respects, they do not mesh with the archaeological record. By most accounts, Catawba reservation life was characterized by indolence (see, e.g., Hutchison 1843; Jones 1815; Mills 1826; Smyth 1784). However, accounts of daily life describe Catawba men away hunting and fishing, or Catawba women busily engaged in pottery production (see, e.g., Jones 1815; Smyth 1784; Watson 1856). This apparent contradiction may be due to the failure of Catawbas—particularly the men—to become civilized yeoman farmers. Catawba men persisted in the "savage" pursuits of hunting and fishing (augmenting the proceeds of commercial activities). Moreover, Catawba men and women funded their "indolent" lifestyle partly through land leasing, an enterprise David Hutchison clearly believed was contributing to Catawba degeneracy. Hutchison was certainly not alone in perceiving land leasing as a corrupting influence. Cherokee men who attempted to rent their land to white sharecroppers were discouraged from doing so by government agents because it might promote "indolent savagery" rather than civilized farming (Perdue 1998:125–126).

European observers tended to characterize Catawba reservation life in terms of abject poverty (see Jones 1815; Mills 1826; Smyth 1784). Yet, contrary to descriptions of destitution, the plethora of goods represented by archaeological assemblages suggests that Catawba families had considerable access to the marketplace.

Archaeological and documentary evidence related to pre-Removal Cherokee households in North Carolina provide a useful comparison. In an exhaustive study of Cherokee ethnicity, Brett Riggs (1999) contrasts the lifeways of Removal-period "mixed blood" or *métis* and traditional Cherokee households. *Métis* Cherokees were often engaged in large-scale surplus agricultural production for market exchange. Wealth generated from this exchange enabled them to acquire "large arrays of commercially manufactured goods, which clearly denote Western modes of domestic and economic life" (Riggs 1999:538). In contrast, traditional Cherokee households were typically engaged in small-scale, subsistence farming, did not participate in the market economy, and possessed "small, low valued assemblages in which traditional technologies are prominent" (Riggs 1999:538).

While the Catawbas at New Town certainly occupied a tenuous position in South Carolina society, they had nevertheless effectively integrated themselves in the market economy, and were able to acquire considerable arrays of Western goods. However, the Catawbas' path to the marketplace was very different from that of the *métis* Cherokees and was viewed by whites as the antithesis of civilized conduct.

Discourse in a Fictional Account of the Catawba Pottery Trade

Patricia Galloway (2006:33) proposes that dearth and bias are the nemeses of ethnohistorians. Accounts of the Catawba, being few in number and short on factual details, are no exception to this axiom. However, if one is interested in the form as well as the content of narratives, one account of the Catawba provides a wealth of information. One short story, "Caloya; or, the Loves of the Driver," written by William Gilmore Simms in 1839, not only provides a window into the conduct of this trade, but also offers important insights into how the Catawba were perceived by white observers at that time.

Simms (1806–70) was the best-known author of the antebellum South. In addition to being a renowned author, he was also a member of the planter class, owning two lowcountry plantations along the Edisto River. In his many stories and novels, he firmly upheld the racial hierarchy of the South; despite his clearly articulated racism, scholars consider his views of American Indians to have been relatively sympathetic for his time (Guilds 2003; Hudson 2003).

Simms freely admits to taking artistic license with certain elements of his Indian writings, particularly Indian myth and religion. However, in terms of background information, Simms claims to have strove for realism; Simms certainly spent more time actually observing Indians than other authors of his day (Hudson 2003:xxxvi–xxxviii).

Nevertheless, what may be understood as realism in Simms's Indian writing is simply the faithful and effective deployment of European racial discourse. As revealed in his writing, Simms's views on Indians fit neatly into the categories outlined in this study: Indians were either wild savages or degraded savages (Simms's essay "North American Indians" [2003b:7–19] is particularly illustrative of his views).

In "The Loves of the Driver," Simms relates his impressions of Catawbas engaged in their pottery trade, which he witnessed as a youth in the vicinity of Charleston (Simms 2003a:218). Simms also appears to incorporate his impressions of the Catawbas on their reservation, which he visited in 1825 (Simms 2003b:15; Simms 2003c:29).

Set in the time of his boyhood (ca. 1815–20), "The Loves of the Driver" features two Catawba characters: a Catawba woman, who is an industrious potter, and her husband, who is a drunken outcast. In portraying these characters, Simms depicted his experiences with the Catawbas using the discursive categories familiar in his day: the woman potter, Caloya, is depicted as a noble and beautiful wild savage engaged in an ancient but dying tradition. She represents Simms's romantic boyhood view of Catawbas traveling, and making and selling pottery in the lowcountry. Her husband, Richard Knuckles, is depicted as indolent, drunken, and "degraded" both in morals and physical appearance; he undoubtedly represents Simms's view of the Catawbas on their reservation in 1825.

In Simms's story, the Catawbas set up their camp on a plantation. The dashing young owner of the plantation welcomes the Indians' arrival, stating that his land is "the place . . . where they have been getting their clay ever since my grandfather settled this plantation . . . I am pleased that they should come to the accustomed place for their clay" (Simms 2003a:224).

During the course of the story, violence erupts between the potter's husband and one of the planter's slaves, a driver named Mingo, who has romantic designs on the potter. The planter acts as a protector to the beautiful potter. In recognition of the planter's benevolent paternalism, the woman presents him with a pair of moccasins and leggings, "neatly made and fancifully decorated with beads" (Simms 2003a: 272–273).

Thus, in addition to representing a planter's view of the Catawba Indians, Simms also provides insights into how planters conceived their own place in the South: worldly and culturally sophisticated (Leath and McInnis 1999), guarantors of the established social order (Joyner 2005:9; Waterhouse 2005:87–88), and paternalistic figures with deep roots in Southern society (Baird 2006).

In describing the Catawbas' pottery and their trade, Simms reveals a clear sympathy for the Catawba as loyal and useful wild savages—precisely the image cultivated by Catawba warriors and anxious colonists during the 18th century. Simms, speaking as narrator, claims that Catawba pottery had long been of value to "the citizens," especially "worthy housewives," among whom it was considered far superior to other wares, and that it was "a confident faith among the old ladies, that okra soup was always inferior if cooked in any but an Indian pot . . . certainly an iron vessel is one of the last which should be employed in the preparation of this truly southern dish" (Simms 2003a:218–219).

This suggests that Catawba pottery had indeed become something of a brand name in parts of 18th- and 19th-century South Carolina. The connection between a "*truly southern dish*" and Catawba pottery, and the willingness of Simms's fictional planter to allow the Catawbas to camp on his land speaks to the nature of the Catawbas' role in white narratives of South Carolina colonial history and culture.

At the time of Simms's writing in 1839, the Catawba Nation was in crisis. After the death of prominent community leader Sally New River in 1820, Catawba society began to fragment. Under pressure from the state legislature, in the late 1830s the Catawbas decided to cede their land to South Carolina and relocate to North Carolina. Simms was presumably aware of these developments. Invoking images of Indian degeneration and the vanishing race, Simms as narrator remarks, "The Catawbas seldom now descend to the seaboard. They have lost the remarkable elasticity of character which particularly distinguished them among the aboriginal nations, and, in declining years and numbers . . . the ancient potteries are almost entirely abandoned . . . I am afraid that I have seen the last of the Indian pots!" (Simms 2003a:219–220).

The cession of Catawba land and relocation of Catawbas to North Carolina certainly influenced Simms's narrative. Nonetheless, Simms's invocation of degraded savagery and the vanishing race is in perfect accord with earlier documentary accounts of life on the Catawba reservation, accounts describing the Catawbas' degeneration and imminent demise that had been appearing since the 1770s (see Jones 1815; Smyth 1784; Watson 1856).

In crafting their accounts of life on the Catawba reservation, the European observers previously cited utilized images of Indian degeneration and the "vanishing race." To any knowledgeable European observer at that time, diminished numbers and sedentary life on a reservation signaled degeneration and extinction as appropriate frames of reference. Although Catawba men continued to hunt and fish, and Catawba women continued to make pottery and baskets, by virtue of their sedentary existence and small population, they were no longer truly wild savages.

What distinguishes Simms's perspectives on the Catawbas from those of earlier observers is his association of Catawba pottery with wild savagery and nomadism and his emphasis on the usefulness of Catawba pottery. John Smyth (1784:124) dismissed Catawba pottery as "ill-formed and half-baked" earthenware, "sold for the most worthless invaluable considerations." Smyth's evaluation of Catawba pottery may simply be a matter of taste; however, Smyth's perspectives on the Catawbas were limited to the Catawba reservation.

Unlike Smyth and Jones, Simms observed Catawba potters *traveling,* "at certain seasons from their far home in the interior to the seaboard," where they "squatted down . . . raised their poles, erected their sylvan tents, and . . . established themselves a temporary abiding place" (Simms 2003a:218). In his narrative, Simms was referring very specifically to pottery traded in the lowcountry, produced by nomadic wild savages, rather than sedentary, degraded savages. Thus, in his visit to the Catawba reservation in 1825, and in the dissolution of the Catawba Nation in 1839, Simms saw degraded savages and a vanishing race, much as did John Smyth in the 1770s. However, Simms interpreted his experience of the pottery trade in the lowcountry, which he witnessed circa 1815, through a different lens—that of wild savagery. The Indians were the same, but the context in which they were observed made for a world of difference.

Conclusion

Paige Raibmon (2005:198) describes aboriginal lives in 19th-century America as "complicated and hard-won blends of indigenous and colonial practices." For better or worse, the Catawba, in their roles as ethnic soldiers, deerskin traders, and itinerant potters—all sophisticated adaptations of indigenous practices to the market economy—were perceived by European observers as exhibiting their "natural" Indian character. In the eyes of whites, the Catawbas were inseparable from the roles they played—and objects they produced—in colonial society. As degenerate Indians no longer performing these roles, their extinction was believed inevitable.

Contrary to Simms's portrayal of a vanishing race, the Catawbas' "ancient potteries" were not abandoned. Although they had largely ceased their itinerant trade, Catawbas continued to make pottery while among the Cherokees in North Carolina, and once reestablished on their reservation, produced pottery that they sold locally throughout the 19th and 20th centuries (Blumer 2004; Fewkes 1944; Harrington 1908; Riggs et al. 2006).

William Gilmore Simms's portrayal of the Catawba encapsulates the power that colonial discourses had over both whites and Indians. At the same time, Simms's narrative demonstrates the Catawbas' success in manipulation of both colonial discourses and institutions. The Catawbas remain in South Carolina, living today not far from where Spanish conquistadors first encountered them in the 1530s (Hudson 1990). Catawbas continue to make pottery, producing artistic wares for the Indian arts and crafts market. Indeed, pottery not only provides Catawbas with a source of income, it remains an important part of Catawba identity.

On his American Indian Pottery website (www.catawbaindianpottery.com), Catawba master potter Marcus Sanders states, "Clay is the life blood of the Catawba Indian Nation. Without clay, there would be no Catawba Nation today." Through his website, Sanders markets his work along with that of the "75 or so adult Catawba potters," who are both his relatives and fellow tribal members. According to Sanders, marketing Catawba pottery online benefits two groups of individuals: "First, the potters who live in absolute obscurity are able to face a world-wide market. Second, Indian pottery collectors can watch this website and find pieces of the quality and the price they can afford and make purchases." Nineteenth-century reports of the Catawbas' imminent demise—and the loss of their "remarkable elasticity of character"—were clearly exaggerated.

Acknowledgments

I would like to thank the Research Laboratories of Archaeology for enabling me to be part of the Catawba project. Vin Steponaitis, Steve Davis, and Brett Riggs have provided invaluable mentoring and support, without which this chapter would not have been possible. I would also like to thank my coeditor, Lance Greene, both for his boundless fortitude in the production of this volume and his feedback on this chapter.

Support for this project was provided in part by a UNC Center for the Study of the American South summer research grant. I would also like to thank the UNC Office of Undergraduate Research; their undergraduate mentoring program provided me with financial support and timely help from Daniel Ladu, a highly capable research assistant.

3 / Identity in a Post-Removal Cherokee Household, 1838–50

Lance Greene

Introduction

By the spring of 1838 over seven thousand federal and state troops were stationed in the Cherokee Nation to prepare for the forced removal of the Cherokees to west of the Mississippi River. The Cherokee Nation in 1838 encompassed parts of Georgia, Alabama, Tennessee, and North Carolina. The segment of the Cherokee population in the mountainous section of southwestern North Carolina was the home of the most traditional and, from the army's perspective, dangerous community in the Cherokee Nation (see Figure 3.1; Finger 1984:20). Many of the federal soldiers in the region had just marched from Florida, where they had participated in America's first guerrilla war, fighting the Seminole Indians who were resisting forced removal. Armed resistance was not contemplated by most Cherokees in the region. However, the vast majority of Cherokees rejected the Treaty of New Echota, the basis for their forced removal. The Cherokee population in North Carolina was composed largely of traditionalists who believed that Chief John Ross could negotiate for permission for them to remain in the state (McLoughlin 1990:152–170; Mooney 1982:129). Despite this belief, many Cherokee families who had decided to remain in the area made contingent plans on how to do so.

Removal of the southern tribes was tied to other major, contemporary events. The most significant of these was the expansion of cotton agriculture and the concomitant growth of racial slavery. Land in the upper South, including that within the Cherokee Nation, was needed for raising crops and livestock to feed the rapidly expanding slave population, the foundation for wealth accumulation in the South (Inscoe 1996:25–58). Therefore, in addition to establishing forts and prisoner of war camps, the army fulfilled another significant function. They created the set-

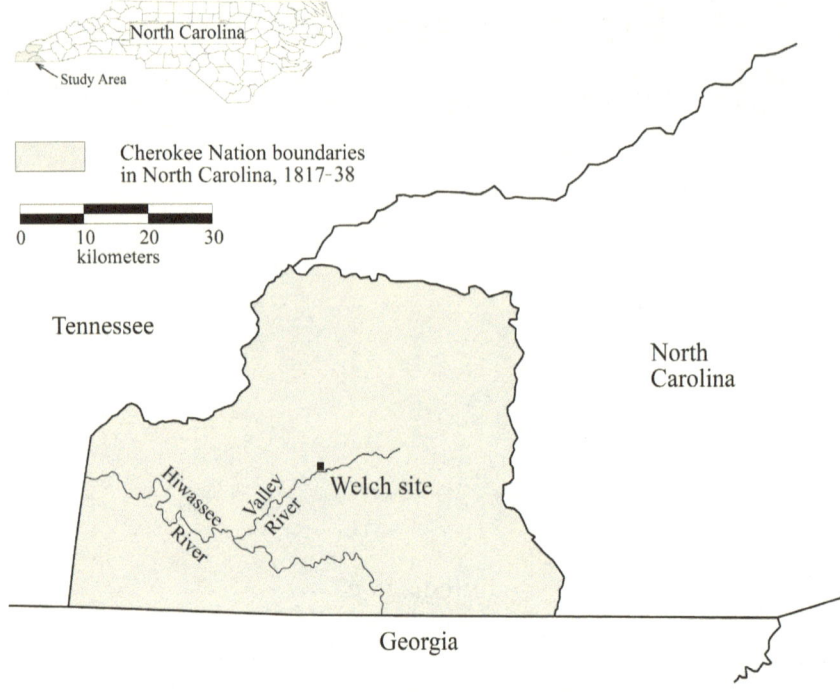

3.1. Location of study area in southwestern North Carolina

ting for modernization of the old Cherokee Nation, by effectively mapping and gridding a relatively unknown block of land within the boundaries of the United States. The forced removal of the southern tribes was, ultimately, about modernization of the land and the people. Anderson (1991) discusses the qualitative changes in forms of governmental control during the shift to modernity during the early to mid 19th century. Foucault, in a similar vein, discusses a contemporaneous shift in powers wielded by the state that impact populations on a deeper, sociological level (Foucault 1978, 1979). Many of the events that occurred within the Cherokee Nation during and after Removal correspond closely with the construction of modernity as posited by Anderson (1991), Calhoun (1994), and Foucault (1978, 1979). The devices used by the army (e.g., maps and censuses) prepared the ground for state control of the lands previously recognized as the Cherokee Nation.

During military occupation (1836–38), army cartographers created detailed topographic maps of the area that show the locations of Cherokee farms as well as valuable natural resources: timber, iron, marble, water, and fertile soil. State control was attempted through the establishment of specific criteria: adequate infrastructure, gridded space (including both people, with the census, and land, with private property), collection of taxes and fees, and ideological constructions of the "other." Thus the military occupation of the Cherokee Nation represented the initiation of new forms of personal control and institutional domination at the "threshold of modernity" (Foucault 1978:143).

Cherokee agent Benjamin Currey described the significance of a census of the Cherokees recorded in 1835: "To be fully possessed of a knowledge of their number, the number of each man's houses, the number of his farms, with the quantity of land under cultivation, the proportion of tillable land, the mineral resources & water privileges of the country&c, the commissioners would be able to fix a true estimate upon the value of the country in case the whole tribe does not approve of the gross sum fixed upon already" (Currey 1835). Currey suggested a detailed list of resources was required in case the Cherokees questioned their federal reimbursement. However, these lists, along with the army survey notes, were invaluable in ranking the quality of tracts sold at the state auction in 1838 and 1839.

Property boundaries were also established. Reuben Deaver, a civilian surveyor, was hired to survey the vacated Cherokee lands in North Carolina; he delineated salable tracts, ranging from 50 to 400 acres. Many of these property boundaries are still in use. During this period a new national form of domination was largely achieved through these forms of control and the identification of "normal" social behavior, thereby creating identifiable "abnormal" or "anomalous" behavior (Foucault 1978, 1979; Rabinow 1984). In the United States this was also the era of a national endeavor to define what was "American." Often this definition was based on those groups who were seen as un-American, such as Indian populations (McLoughlin 1990:4–6).

Historically, such modernization efforts have been largely successful. However, people often find ways to subvert these powerful forces. This is particularly true in certain settings, such as during periods of the establishment of a state. These instances, usually defined with discrete temporal and geographic boundaries, have been variously termed liminal spaces, borderlands, the frontier, the periphery, and the middle ground (Adelman and Aron 1999; Haefeli 1999; Lightfoot and Martinez 1995; van Gennep 1960; White 1991). This chapter investigates one such attempt to subvert these military, and later, civilian, efforts to make people, Indian, black, and white, conform to a national ideal. This subversion was an incredible achievement, given it was against two of the most overtly powerful and violent aspects of modernity—military occupation and state expansion.

Historical Narrative of the Welch Family

Two individuals who avoided removal and helped others to do so were John and Elizabeth Welch. John was a Cherokee man and Elizabeth, or Betty, was a white woman, a member of a family who had lived within the Cherokee Nation for decades (Jurgelski 2004). Archival records show that the couple supported dozens, perhaps hundreds, of Cherokees hiding in the mountains during the removal efforts (Bynum 1838; Porter 1838). This research focuses on how the Welches managed to remain in North Carolina and helped reestablish a traditional community, against the explicit orders of the United States Government. First is a discussion of this period in the history of the Welch family as described by the documentary evidence, and then a discussion of the archaeological data and the contribution they make to this research.

In treaties with the United States in 1817 and 1819, the Cherokees ceded a large tract of land north of the Little Tennessee River in North Carolina to the United States. Specific acts in these treaties stated that Cherokee families could acquire 640 acres from these ceded lands, if they chose to sever ties with the Cherokee Nation and accept U.S. citizenship. Much to the chagrin of many officials, numerous Cherokee families, including the Welches, accepted this offer. However, within five years most of these families had been bought out or forcibly removed by white settlers flooding into the newly acquired land (Jurgelski 2004). Most of the Cherokee "reservees" then moved back into the Cherokee Nation. As a result of these events, the Welches moved to the Valley River area of southwestern North Carolina in the early 1820s (see Figure 3.1). There they quickly established a large-scale farm and, by the 1830s, were wealthy landowners. At the time of Removal, the Welch family was comfortably situated, with more than one hundred acres under cultivation by eight black slaves and a number of white tenants (Browder 1973). The 1837 federal property appraisals indicate that the Welches lived in a 40-foot-long hewn-log house and operated, among other undertakings, a gristmill (Welch and Jarrett 1838). The majority of the Welch's wealth lay in free-ranging livestock; Welch's son-in-law, John Powell (an officer in the Tennessee militia), testified that the family was the largest stockholder in southwestern North Carolina (Powell 1843).

Because John Welch had been "citizenized" as a reservee in 1819 and the family included a white woman who was a citizen of the state of North Carolina, the family obtained a special exemption from Removal. As the forced military removal became inevitable, the Welches made preparations to consolidate their holdings and remain in the Valley River region. Yet when the soldiers actually began the removal operations, the Welches initiated acts of resistance that endangered their own increasingly tenuous status. Army correspondence reveals that the Welches were responsible for hiding and feeding numerous Cherokees resisting capture during the summer and fall of 1838. On June 13, 1838, the commander at Fort Montgomery reported: "I collected yesterday about 80 Indians. They had all received orders from Welch on Valley River to leave home & take to the mountains" (Lieutenant Colonel John Gray Bynum, June 13, 1838). A week later, an officer reported: "I have, with my company, taken post here convenient to two points [one of which is Welch's, the other Colvard's] where the Indians are fed and harboured and where the trails from the mountains, on both sides of the river, concentrate.... Welch's family and Nancy Colvard... should be apprehended and sent in... Welch's people I understand have liberty from Genl. Eustis. These two families are doing a great deal of mischief" (Captain G. Porter, June 18, 1838).

The army viewed the Welches as extremely dangerous, and near the end of removal John Welch was held illegally in prison, where he became seriously ill. When Welch was finally released in November 1838, he was blinded by infection and never recovered his physical health (Powell 1843). When most of the Cherokee Nation was marched westward, John was allowed to return home. When Welch returned to Valley River, he found that "Florada [sic] soldiers with a horde of equally worthless white men rioting in and plundering of his property" had stripped his farm (Welch 1843). The Welches were not removed, but, in addition to the ransacking of their farm, they were forced to purchase their own land. On November 2, 1838, while John Welch was still imprisoned, John Powell attended the state auction. He purchased the farm, roughly 12 hundred acres, for $8,000, providing a $1,000 cash down payment. A year later, in November 1839, Powell transferred all of the deeds to Betty (Cherokee County Register of Deeds 1839).

With property ownership reestablished, the Welches were able to help recreate a traditional Cherokee community, based on a patron-client relationship. The Cherokee families they had helped hide during Removal returned to the Valley River area, where many rebuilt a community on Welch land, which soon became known as Welch's Town. Documentary records suggest the Cherokee families that lived on the Welch farm tended livestock for the Welches, but reveal little else regarding the economic aspects of their relationship. Local inhabitants as well as historians have debated whether the Welches, and a small number of other patrons, in assisting the Cherokees during and after Removal, were motivated by altruism or capitalist pursuits (e.g., Finger 1984; Godbold and Russell 1990; Russell 1956).

Existence was very tenuous for the Cherokees; the novel environment of the post-Removal era made it impossible for either Cherokees or Cherokee agents to know who was there legally or illegally. The Cherokees were not state or federal citizens and landownership was in question. For at least a decade following Removal they were in constant fear of a second removal. Federal agents made numerous attempts to achieve "voluntary emigration" in an effort to rid the state of all those of Cherokee ancestry (Finger 1984).

Because John was legally barred from landownership and his health was in serious decline, Betty became the leader, at least publicly, of Welch's Town. In 1841 she turned away a government agent, Thomas Hindman, who was bent on effecting a second "voluntary" removal of the remaining Cherokees in North Carolina. Hindman's frustrated efforts are revealed in numerous letters to his superiors in which he denounced Betty as a shrewd and cunning adversary:

> This settlement are principally full blood Cherokees and completely subservient to the will of Mrs. Welch, a white woman (wife of John Welch, Cherokee) and she, under the influence of Mr. Thomas. Mrs. Welch has considerable shrewdness and understands how to manage ignorant Indians to suit her purpose. She has purchased some twelve or thirteen hundred acres of land from the state of North Carolina at something near the sum of $8000 . . . The largest portion of the Indians are settled upon this land . . . She spares no pains to keep up their prejudices against the West and tells them they can always have the priviledges of working her land and residing upon it. [Hindman 1841]

In 1844 Betty intervened on behalf of the Welch's Town Cherokees by abruptly stopping the efforts of J. W. King, a local businessman, to purchase their claims against the government at a fraction of their value. In correspondence regarding the incident he referred to her as the "Demon in Human Shape" (King 1844). These activities are representative of the unusual power Betty wielded as a married woman in the antebellum period. Her interaction with King occurred four years before the Married Women's Property Act in New York. The act, the result of years of effort by reformers such as Elizabeth Cady Stanton, attempted to curb the complete loss of legal rights of married women under the common-law tradition of *femme covert*. This tradition withheld the rights of married women to own property, acquire wealth, write a will or other contract, or sue, in their own name (Skinner 1996:90–91). Betty's control of the property was also coincident with the spread of the cult of domesticity. This ideology stressed the role of women as nurturers who belonged in a domestic setting, away from the arena of business and politics (Boydston 1990; Cott 1977; Welter 1966). Betty may have been one of the few married women in the American South at the time who not only owned and controlled property, but interacted on an equal footing with government officials and business elites. This was made feasible partly by Betty's marriage to a nonwhite man, which was in itself another negation of a supposedly inviolable social contract.

Betty's power to negotiate these matters depended, ironically, on the Cherokee community she and John were trying to protect. There was a severe labor shortage in the region, and the Welches were lucky enough, or astute enough, to have held onto a labor force of roughly 50 Cherokee adults (Siler 1972; Thomas 1840). They successfully used the liminal space of the post-Removal era to simultaneously maintain their farm and wealth and re-create a traditional Cherokee community for those who had determined they would not be forced from their homeland. Much of the land purchased by the Welches after Removal was in the steep mountains above the Valley River, where the families of Welch's Town could rebuild their community in relative isolation from local whites. This was an important consideration, for increasing racism, polarized on a white/nonwhite axis, was expressed openly about the Cherokees who had remained in the region. A statement in 1840 by a local white farmer, Andrew Barnard, summarizes both the efforts of the Welch community and the feelings of some of the local whites. Barnard seethed: "[They are] forming Settlements, building town houses, and Show every disposition to keep up their former manners and customs of councils, dances, ballplays, and other practices, which is disgusting to civilized Society and calculated to corrupt our youth, and produce distress and confusion among all good thinking people" (Barnard 1840).

While the members of Welch's Town chose to retain these aspects of traditional identity, the Welches embraced certain aspects of modernity. They produced large surpluses of crops and livestock and owned several African American slaves. They supported construction of the Western Turnpike in the 1850s, which ran within two hundred feet of their house. Maps of the Valley River Valley, drawn in 1850 and 1860, show numerous European American houses, and a small number of Cherokee houses, including the Welches, located along the turnpike. However, the bulk of Cherokee houses are conspicuously absent from these maps, suggesting they were set away from the turnpike, removed from the travelers' gaze. For the Welches, subversion of modernization largely meant maintaining local communities and local governance. However, they didn't reject the accumulation of surplus wealth or African American slavery; they had participated in these prior to Removal.

Archaeological Investigations of the Welch Site

In the summer of 2003 a group of archaeologists, including myself, from the University of North Carolina and Appalachian State University, located the Welch house site. During shovel test excavations, a cluster of subsurface pits was identified. A small block area was excavated, exposing three aligned, substructure cellar pits (see Figure 3.2). These were probably subjacent to an external kitchen which is described in the 1838 army spoliation claims. The three pits were excavated in the summer of 2004. Each pit contained three to four well-defined strata. The fill in each pit contained a large amount and variety of domestic artifacts and food remains. Ceramic refits between the various strata and pits suggest these deposits represent a short-term depositional event dating to about 1850.

The ceramic assemblage consists of 642 sherds; analysis identified a minimum of 108 food preparation, storage, and serving vessels (see Table 3.1). The vast majority of ceramics are whiteware sherds. Much smaller numbers of yellowware, ironstone, redware, creamware, and alkaline-glazed stoneware sherds were also recovered. The calculation of minimum number of vessels is commonly used by historic archaeologists and considered to provide a more realistic account of ceramics used by site occupants than sherd counts (Miller 1991a).

3.2. Substructure cellar pit excavation at the Welch site

During the early to mid 19th century, relatively inexpensive and widely available utilitarian ceramics (as well as higher status wares) were widely produced in England (Miller 1991b). Whiteware, with a wide variety of decorative styles, was the ceramic form used on a daily basis by most ethnic groups and by all economic classes during this period. It is one of the few ceramic wares that appears in almost all archaeological assemblages from the period (e.g., Burley et al. 1992; Lightfoot et al. 1998; Riggs 1996; Schurr 2006). The most inexpensive versions were undecorated, but ceramics with printed scenes or painted edges were becoming less expensive (Miller 1991b). Transfer-printed pieces were the most expensive decorative whiteware form at the time (Miller 1991a:12–22).

A variety of decorations was present on whiteware sherds recovered from the Welch site, including blue and green shell-edged, transfer-printed, dipped, hand-painted, and sponge-decorated types. These decorative styles, with the exception of transfer-printing, have been identified as some of the cheapest ceramic wares available at the time (Miller 1991b). Indeed, the ceramic assemblage from the Welch site is in many ways very similar to that of two nearby contemporary sites. The McCombs site (1848–65) is located near the Hiwassee River, roughly 15 kilometers south of the Welch site. Excavations at McCombs uncovered the remains of three slave cabins (Shumate et al. 2000). While ceramics were a much smaller portion of the total assemblage (19 percent), the composition of the ceramic assem-

3.1. Minimum number of ceramic vessels by decorative style, Welch site

Decoration	plate	cup	saucer	bowl	platter	mug	creamer	sugar bowl	gravy boat	churn	crock	unidentified	TOTAL
shell-edged	30	0	0	0	0	0	0	0	0	0	0	0	30
hand-painted	3	8	9	3	0	1	1	0	1	0	0	0	26
transfer-printed	3	2	2	6	0	0	0	0	0	0	0	1	14
sponge-decorated	1	0	2	0	0	0	0	0	0	0	0	0	3
dipped	0	0	0	1	0	1	0	0	0	0	0	4	6
luster-glazed	0	0	0	1	0	0	0	0	0	0	0	0	1
alkaline-glazed	0	0	0	0	0	0	0	0	0	1	6	0	7
undecorated	3	3	5	6	1	0	0	1	0	0	0	2	21
TOTAL	40	13	18	17	1	2	1	1	1	1	6	7	108

blage is very similar to that of the Welch site. Whiteware sherds comprise the bulk of the ceramic assemblage, and are represented by undecorated, transfer-printed, hand-painted, shell-edged, dipped, and sponge-decorated wares. Much smaller numbers of pearlware, creamware, stoneware, porcelain, semi-porcelain, and bone china were also recovered (Shumate et al. 2000:7.4). The Hawkins-Sourjohn site (ca. 1860) is located along the Valley River, 16 kilometers downstream from the Welch site. A single cellar pit, associated with a white tenant family, was excavated at the site. Ceramics recovered from the pit include numerous whiteware sherds (including undecorated, transfer printed, hand painted, shell edged, spatter, and sponge decorated) and a small number of stoneware, pearlware, yellowware, and coarse earthenware sherds (Riggs 1996).

Alkaline-glazed stoneware sherds were recovered from all three sites. These wares were used mainly for food production and storage. Common vessel forms include open-mouthed jars and constricted-rim jugs; volumes range from one pint to over five gallons (Zug 1986:285–318). During the mid 19th century, the mountain and piedmont regions of North Carolina were home to several centers of alkaline-glazed stoneware production (Zug 1986). Yellowware vessels, designed for food preparation and serving, were produced in the United States by the 1830s (Ramsay 1947:148). Yellowwares were made with few decorations and were probably cheaper than whitewares during this period (Miller 1991b:48). Undecorated ironstone, which was gaining popularity at mid-century, and which was more expensive than most whitewares (Miller 1991a:9, 12–22), is represented by only six sherds at the Welch site. The assemblage contains no porcelain or bone china.

Numerous pieces of flatware were recovered, including two- and three-tine forks, table knives, and spoons. Most of the knives and forks have retained their bone or antler handles. Many of the utensils had been repaired; bone was cut and fitted by members of the Welch farm to replace original bone handles broken during use. A small number of glass fragments from the Welch site represents olive-green bottles or flasks, drinking glasses, pitchers, and medicine vials.

Artifacts related to dining (ceramics, glassware, utensils; n = 732) reveal a household in which Western items were widely used. Absent from the Welch assemblage are the higher-status items such as porcelain, bone china, and pressed glass; in addition, there was considerable utensil repair. A dining assemblage of much higher status would certainly have been possible for the Welches, given their wealth and the availability of such goods at local outlets (Thomas 1839–42). This assemblage, largely utilitarian, was the result of conscious choices by the Welches. These choices reflect their acceptance of westernized materials but also a rejection of certain aspects of wealth display. Thus, in rejecting the trappings of the southern plantation mistress, Betty disavowed many of the values of westernized society. This rejection derived in part from continued associations with the members of Welch's Town, who still adhered to a communal ethos in which displays of wealth were strongly discouraged.

Also present were several items associated with clothing production and maintenance, including brass pins, small brass hooks and eyelets, cloth fragments, and brass, bone, pewter, and iron buttons. Local store ledgers from this period reveal the Welches purchased large amounts of cloth, buttons, and brass pins (Thomas 1839–42). Given the variety of clothing items in the archaeological record and ledger accounts, it is probable that members of the Welch farm were producing clothes not only for their use but for sale as well. It is unknown if this production was performed by Cherokees, whites, or blacks; however, it was most likely performed by women (Hill 1997). A substantial proportion of the farm income may have been acquired through such work.

Another class of artifacts represents both gender and ethnicity: carved and polished stone. Several pieces of worked stone, including a chlorite-schist pipe and pipe fragments, stone disks, and carved talc, were recovered from the three cellar pits (see Figure 3.3). The stone pipe and fragments were carved from small, locally available schist cobbles that generally occur at rock outcrops along river or stream banks. A knife was used to carve, scrape, and drill these relatively soft schist blocks into small pipes. The forms recovered from the Welch site conform to traditional styles of pipes that had been produced by Cherokees in the region for generations (Adair 1930:455; Riggs 1996; Setzler and Jennings 1941; Witthoft 1949). For John Welch, smoking a carved-stone pipe was an intimate statement for those within the household and for the Cherokees of Welch's Town. While many of Betty's statements through material culture were directed at the outside world, John's statements were a connection to traditional Cherokee beliefs and principles. This was increasingly the case after the removal, at which time Betty became the primary leader of the farm, and John played a lesser role in external affairs.

Similar to stone pipes, carved-stone disks are commonly found on Cherokee sites from the early and mid 19th century. These small, tabular river pebbles were carved or polished on the edges to make them smooth and circular. They were used in the Cherokee basket game, in which teams usually competed for small prizes such as meals or firewood (Freeman-Witthoft 1988). The game has considerable historical depth for the Cherokees, and similar carved-stone and ceramic disks have been recovered from historic and prehistoric sites in the region (Riggs 2000; Riggs et al. 1998; Setzler and Jennings 1941).

This broad array of hand-carved goods from the Welch site, pipes, disks, and unidentified objects, in conjunction with evidence of stone working on site (i.e., items broken during manufacture), may be an indicator of Cherokee ethnicity in the mountains of North Carolina at mid-century. Such collections have been recovered from Removal and post-Removal-era Cherokee sites, such as the Chewkee-

3.3. Chlorite-schist pipe from the Welch site

askee, John Christie, and Lemmons Branch sites (Riggs 1999; Riggs et al. 2001). However, such collections, with evidence of on-site stone working, are absent from contemporary African and European American sites, such as the McCombs and Hawkins-Sourjohn sites (Riggs 1999; Shumate et al. 2000).

Another interesting aspect of the assemblage is the absence of handmade Cherokee pottery, termed the Qualla series by archaeologists. Forerunners of handmade Cherokee ceramics date to the 15th century (Dickens 1979; Ward and Davis 1999: 178–179). The later styles of Qualla ceramics were usually check stamped; this surface treatment dates from roughly 1750 to 1910 or later (Fewkes 1944; Harrington 1908; Riggs 1996:103). Assemblages from several Removal-era sites excavated near the Welch site, including the house site of a wealthy Cherokee family, contained a large number of Qualla sherds (Riggs 1999). During the 19th century, the most common Qualla ceramic vessel form was a large open-mouthed jar. These jars were used to store *kanohena,* or sour corn mush (Riggs 1996:105). They were placed at the front door of Cherokee cabins, and visitors were welcome to eat from the jar. This traditional form of welcome was rejected by the Welch household. It is unknown if this action reflects a rejection of certain forms of Cherokee tradition or, alternatively, a perceived need to downplay any association with Cherokee culture.

The food remains may be the most interesting part of the assemblage. Both floral and faunal remains are well preserved and contain a rich diversity. Domesticated species represented in the cellar pits include cow, pig, sheep, chicken, corn, wheat, rye, barley, oats, rice, apple, peach, watermelon, beans, squash, sunflower, tobacco, and coffee. Wild species include deer, turkey, bear, rabbit, raccoon, squirrel, bass, mallard, bobwhite, snapping turtle, chestnut, hazelnut, hickory nut, acorn, walnut, honey locust, amaranth, elderberry, grape, and bulrush. This diverse array of foods reveals the multitude of tasks performed by the workers, enslaved and free, on the Welch farm. It is probable that the Cherokees of Welch's Town, living in the uplands, were engaged in working small plots of land, and tending hogs and cattle and gathering wild plants and animals. Cherokees had been performing these subsistence practices in the mountains for decades (Klinck and Talman 1970; Riggs 1999:208–216). While upland Cherokees were most likely the source of wild foods, members of the Welch family and their slaves, living along the valley floor of Valley River, were probably responsible for agricultural production of corn, wheat, oats, rye, and other crops. Imported goods such as rice and coffee were readily purchased at the Thomas store nearby (Thomas 1839–42).

First and foremost the food remains suggest that the Welches were eating better than anyone else in the region. The occupants of Welch's Town not only provided them with great financial gain by tending their livestock, they provided wild foods, also, making it possible for the Welches to have a rich and diverse diet. The food remains also speak to the broader question of cultural identity. In previous research I have suggested that, while individuals certainly may alter the material culture related to dining, they often maintain many traditional aspects of their diet (Greene 2005). Although the Welches chose not to have Qualla vessels in their house, they continued to eat traditional foods, in addition to the agricultural products that most local whites commonly consumed. Food remains may be the best indicator of ethnicity, perhaps because the practices and materials associated with dining are often easier to change than what is actually being consumed. In this setting, the food itself is the significant cultural marker. The food remains indicate Betty's willingness to embrace certain aspects of Cherokee tradition. However, the limits of her acceptance of cultural diversity are illustrated by the family's continued ownership of African American slaves.

Conclusion

For the Cherokees who remained in North Carolina, the decade following Removal was a period of immense change, a transitional period in which they maintained no formal tribal government and no clear citizenship. While this marginalization challenged them in many ways, it also provided opportunities to evade governmental, business, and social prejudices. The members of Welch's Town were dependent on each other for social and economic support in the racialized climate of the antebellum South, but they felt secure enough to reestablish a townhouse, stickball fields, and dance grounds. In this sense patronage succeeded in allowing the Cherokees to remain in their homeland and maintain crucial elements of Cherokee culture. Part of the strategy for the Welch family was to outwardly demonstrate their participation in modern westernized lifestyles, but within the boundaries of their farm to maintain a space for the continuation of traditional cultural practices.

The archaeological assemblages recovered from the Welch site provide a unique perspective on the lives of the Welch family. Materiality, although fraught with evidentiary constraints, provides a clear gaze into their daily lives. The remains of what they ate and ate with, what they wore, and what kinds of houses they lived in, go beyond the documents and provide a sense of their lives in relation to others and how they saw themselves. The documentary history of the Welches has allowed me to re-create the context of cultural resistance, but it is the archaeology that has defined what aspects of modernity the Welches embraced, how they presented themselves in the new social terrain of the post-Removal era, and how they helped reconstruct a traditional Cherokee community.

Acknowledgments

I would like to thank several institutions for their generous support that, through the following programs, funded the fieldwork at the Welch site: the Wenner-Gren Foundation Fieldwork Grant, the North Carolina Archaeological Society Grant-in-Aid Program, the University of North Carolina Center for the Study of the American South Summer Research Grant, and the University of North Carolina Research Laboratories of Archaeology Timothy P. Mooney Fellowship. I would also like to thank Mark R. Plane for his tireless efforts as coeditor, and Brett Riggs for sharing his substantial knowledge of eastern Cherokee history and archaeology. Jim and Jeanette Wilson and Burke West have been extremely patient and cooperative during several years of fieldwork on their land, and their enthusiasm for local history has resulted in many interesting conversations. Input from members of the Eastern Band of Cherokee Indians has been very informative and has guided the ways in which I approach Cherokee archaeology.

4 / Business in the Hinterlands
The Impact of the Market Economy on the West-Central Great Plains at the Turn of the 19th Century
Cody Newton

Introduction

The expansion of European settlers across the North American continent was preceded by the movement of European goods. Although the implications of direct physical contact between Indian groups and Europeans are better documented, there is little doubt that indirect contact, through the acquisition of European technologies and the impacts of epidemic disease, affected Indian demographics and cultural landscapes. However, in areas such as the west-central Great Plains, largely unexplored or settled by Europeans until the 19th century, Indian societies were able to maintain, for the most part, a pre-contact existence well into the 19th century.

Using archaeological evidence from two post-contact sites in the Lykins Valley of north-central Colorado in conjunction with documentary evidence, this chapter addresses the degree to which Indian groups on the western margin of the Great Plains were affected by European market economies. Specifically, material assemblages from the Lykins Valley site (5LR263) and images from a nearby rock art site (5LR293), combined with contextual historical data, will be used to show the degree that European market economies impacted Indian groups in the region. This analysis demonstrates that the American Indian occupants of Lykins Valley maintained traditional technologies, subsistence practices, and quite possibly, group identity as a consequence of their distance from the direct impacts of European markets.

Beyond the Valley: European and Indian Groups in Regional Context

Documented accounts from the 16th through 18th centuries provide no evidence of European exploration near Lykins Valley. However, these accounts show the large-scale trends of exploration into the region. From the initial Spanish *entradas* through the later French and American expeditions, encroachment into the region increased (see Table 4.1). Undoubtedly preceded by earlier, undocumented trappers and traders, Major Steven Long led the first documented expedition into northern Colorado. Long traveled up the South Platte River, passing the mouth of the Cache la Poudre River on July 3, 1820, before continuing south along the Front Range to the Arkansas River (Benson 1988). There is no direct account of Lykins Valley at this time and Boxelder Creek does not appear on a map until 1845 (Frémont 1845). Accounts from the Long expedition, compiled by expedition member Edwin James, indicate that, at that time, the Cache la Poudre River was frequented by a band of Kiowa (Benson 1988:198). Other historic accounts document the Arapaho used the Cache la Poudre Valley as a hunting ground and often camped on Boxelder Creek (Watrous 1911:15).

The movement of these groups was widespread and the dispersal and coalescence of different tribal groups on the plains during this period often resulted in camps being composed of individuals from many different tribes. Edwin James describes a location on the South Platte at the mouth of Cherry Creek near present-day Denver where a mixed group of Kiowa, Kiowa-Apache, and Arapaho had a rendezvous for trade with the Cheyenne (Benson 1988:202). Groups were known to travel great distances from their home territories. The Comanche, for example, visited the Green River Rendezvous in southwestern Wyoming during the early 19th century (Keyser et al. 2004:136). An Arapaho group traveled to the Saskatchewan River to trade at the Chesterfield House in 1801 in the company of their kin, the Gros Ventre (Binnema 2001:171).

The Mexican Revolution of 1821 and the resulting expulsion of the Spanish from New Mexico paved the way for uncontested trade in the plains and mountains of western North America. The fur-trade era (1824–40) was a time of increased trade, requiring an infrastructure of trading establishments to facilitate this exchange. Numerous trading establishments appeared all over the west and provided points of contact between trappers and traders. In the western plains of Colorado, the fur trade began around 1830 and resulted in the construction of numerous competing trade forts or posts along the Front Range and on the Western Slope. Beginning with the establishment of Fort Uncompahgre in 1829, at least 21 trading forts or posts were in operation at various times until 1860 in the west-central Great Plains and central Rocky Mountains (cf. Eddy 1982; Robertson 1999). Four of these posts were located along a 20-kilometer stretch of the South Platte River roughly 90 kilometers from Lykins Valley and were in operation from 1835 to 1845. If the Lykins Valley site was occupied during the fur-trade era, it is expected that the trade-goods assemblage would reflect the variety of items available, especially beads (since the site has a relatively large sample), as the variety and quantity of beads inventoried at nearby Fort Jackson would indicate (Peterson 1974:138–

4.1. Exploration into the Great Plains region

Nation	Explorers	Expedition began	Nearest to Lykins Valley (km)	Reference
Spain	Coronado	1540	559 [a]	Lavender (1992)
	Oñate	1601	503 [a]	Schroeder (1962)
	Ulibarri	1706	378 [a]	Thomas (1935)
	Valverde	1719	350 [a]	Thomas (1935)
	Villasur	1720	308 [a]	Weber (1992)
	Anza	1779	312 [a]	Weber (1992)
France	Mallet	1739	510 [a]	Blakeslee (1995)
	Vérendrye	1742	415 [b]	Smith (1980)
United States	Pike	1806	185 [a]	Flores (2005)
	Long	1820	75 [c]	Benson (1988)
	Ashley	1824	27 [d]	Carter (1965)
	Frémont	1842	45 [e]	Burris (2006)
		1843	13 [f]	Burris (2006)

[a] This value based on generally accepted route ± 80 kilometers.
[b] Whether the brothers actually made it to the Bighorn Mountains versus the Black Hills is disputed.
[c] The closest point of the South Platte to Lykins Valley.
[d] Based on journal of camping on and subsequent journey up the Cache la Poudre River onto the Laramie Plains.
[e] This value based on generally accepted route ± 20 kilometers.
[f] Based on journey up the North Fork of the Cache la Poudre River onto the Laramie Plains.

150). Furthermore, the origins of the trade items at the site reflect earlier French and English trade in the region.

Understanding when the site was occupied is important to discerning what Indian group was in Lykins Valley at the time. However, given the homogeneity in the archaeological record of Plains equestrian groups and the number of Indian societies documented in the area during the turn of the 19th century, this identification becomes difficult. The large number of potential Indian groups occupying the Lykins Valley was the result of increasing group mobility, fragmentation, and reorganization under the pressure of European expansion and epidemic disease. Consequently, the Indian group or groups that occupied the region could potentially represent a variety of cultural affiliations (see Table 4.2).

Lykins Valley

Lykins Valley is located on the western margin of the Colorado Piedmont region of the Great Plains and is drained by the South Platte River. The Lykins Valley site

4.2. Known Indian groups in the Lykins Valley vicinity

Date (A.D.)	Groups within 150 km of Lykins Valley	Reference
1600–1700	Comanche	Burris (2006)
	Plains Apache	Bamforth (1988); Scheiber (2006)
	Shoshoni	Bamforth (1988)
	Ute	Bamforth (1988); Burris (2006)
1700–1800	Comanche	Bamforth (1988); Burris (2006)
	Kiowa	Burris (2006)
	Shoshoni	Bamforth (1988)
	Ute	Bamforth (1988)
1800–1860	Arapaho	Bamforth (1988); Burris (2006); Watrous (1911)
	Cherokee	Watrous (1911)
	Cheyenne	Bamforth (1988); Benson (1988); Burris (2006)
	Comanche	Benson (1988)
	Kiowa	Benson (1988)
	Kiowa-Apache	Benson (1988); Burris (2006)
	Pawnee	Watrous (1911)
	Plains Sioux	Burris (2006)
	Ute	Burris (2006)

is an open, stratified campsite located on the alluvial terrace of Boxelder Creek, a small perennial stream (see Figure 4.1). The valley from which the site takes its name is formed by a hogback ridge to the east and the rising mountain slopes of the Laramie Range to the west. The site is located in a plains–foothills ecotone, protected from exposure to the weather extremes common in the mountains and plains (Travis 1988:171). Shelter provided by the valley, along with the water and forage found within the riparian zone of Boxelder Creek, would have made this location favorable for year-round habitation. Immediately north of the site, a small (1,790-hectare) basin bounded by the High Plains scarp was used historically by ranchers to winter livestock because of its sheltered nature and abundant forage, indicating that prey species (i.e., mule deer, pronghorn, bison) would have been in proximity to the site throughout the year.

In a regional context, Lykins Valley was part of a hinterland devoid of significant European encroachment until the first quarter of the 19th century. Neither France nor Spain occupied this area of the Great Plains in the 17th and 18th centuries, though the influx of French traders and trade goods into the Central Plains elicited Spanish responses (most notably the campaign of Villasur in 1720). The overall pattern of French and Spanish interaction involved northeast-southwest

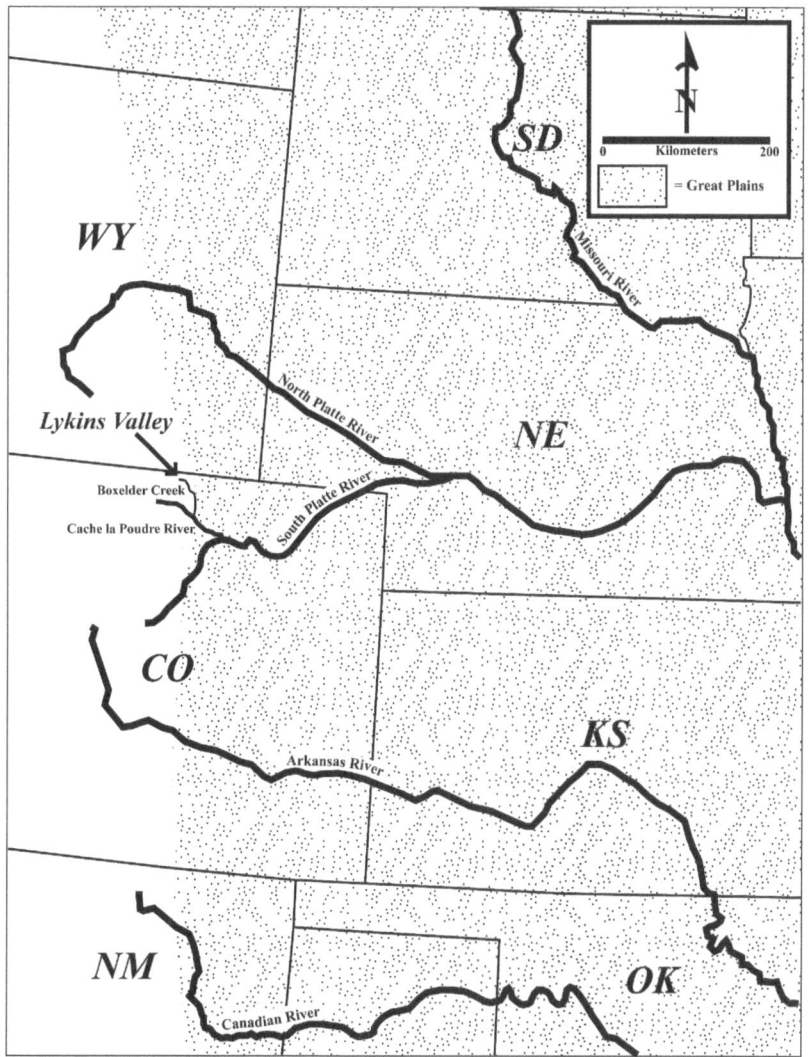

4.1. Location of Lykins Valley

movements that relegated the Lykins Valley area to the periphery. Following the Louisiana Purchase of 1803, European American exploration of the Great Plains, particularly the expeditions of Pike and Freeman-Custis in 1806, met with Spanish resistance (Weber 1992). It was not until after the Mexican Revolution of 1821 that European Americans, mainly trappers and traders, entered the region in any sustained manner.

The Lykins Valley site was excavated in 1974 by archaeologists from Colorado State University (Ohr et al. 1979). The post-contact component of the site consists of 1,533 faunal specimens, 621 lithic artifacts, along with a small but robust

4.3. Post-contact radiocarbon dates and isotopic data from the Lykins Valley site

Sample	Level	Depth (cm)	Description	Material	Reference	$\delta^{13}C$	$\delta^{15}N$	BP	Pooled/calibrated date range[a]
UGa-816	1	0–5	thermal feature	charcoal	Ohr et al. (1979)			250+85	A.D. 1724–1815 (52.7%)
Beta-220556	1		horse metapodial	bone collagen	Newton (2008)	–11.9		170+40	
UGa-813	2	5–10	thermal feature	charcoal	Ohr et al. (1979)			210+95	
Beta-220557	2		horse scapula	bone collagen	Newton (2008)	–16.9	7.1	150+40	A.D. 1731–1808 (57.2%)
Beta-220558	2		bison mandible	bone collagen	Newton (2008)	–8.7		240+40	

[a] All five dates are statistically contemporaneous ($\chi^2 = 3.347$, $p < 0.05$). Here they are pooled by level and the two sigma date range with the highest probability is given.

trade-goods assemblage comprised of a single gunflint, 458 glass beads, *dentalium*, brass kettle parts, a tinkler, a clay pipe, and other unidentified metal fragments. The diversity of these items and the divergent technologies present indicate that an indigenous group using both stone tools and European trade items occupied the site.

The post-contact assemblage was recovered from the surface and from two excavated stratigraphic levels that were originally interpreted as a reoccupation by Plains Apache groups (Ohr et al. 1979:46). However, this interpretation is based on the use of uncalibrated radiocarbon dates (see Table 4.3). Reanalysis of the trade-goods assemblage indicates that the site could not have been occupied until much later, making the determination of ethnic identity much more difficult (see additional discussion below).

Reanalysis of the site spatial data also calls into question whether there were multiple occupations at the site. A plan view map collapsing the two buried occupation levels onto a single surface reveals that artifact concentrations between the levels have very little spatial overlap, and are more representative of a single occupation on a sloped surface (see Figure 4.2).

Analysis of the artifacts represented in Figure 4.2 shows that significant differences exist in the frequencies of artifact types by grid ($G = 66.876$, $df = 4$, $p < 0.001$). Freeman-Tukey deviates, which center on zero and identify values varying significantly from that expected by the null hypothesis, reveal that bone and lithics are overrepresented in Grid 1 whereas European items (i.e., glass beads, clay pipe fragments, metal fragments, and a tinkler cone) are overrepresented in Grids 2 and 3. Underrepresentation of bone in Grid 2 and European items in Grid 1 substantiate the visual pattern evident on the map and indicate that a bone and large-size debitage discard area south of the hearths is present in Grid 1. The European items (especially the beads and tinkler) found in proximity to the hearth in Grids 2 and 3 probably represent artifacts that were lost rather than discarded. The lack of habitation features indicates this was an outside activity area, very similar spatially to the men's outside hearth model described by Binford (1983). The patterning of the artifacts indicates that the discard areas and activity zones generally conform to the prevailing north to northwest wind in the valley, which in this open setting would have dictated sitting on the north/northwest side of the hearth to avoid blowing smoke.

A single occupation is also substantiated by conjoining artifact fragments recovered from the stratigraphic levels (e.g., clay pipe fragments from the surface and level 1, kettle lug fragments from level 1 and 2) and certain artifact classes (e.g., glass trade beads) found in all levels. The amount of weathering on the bone was correlated to size ($n = 1,240$, $rs = 0.109$, $p < 0.001$; the larger specimens, particularly the bison bone, being more weathered), yet was not significantly correlated between levels ($n = 1,240$, $rs = 0.024$, $p = 0.391$), indicating that the faunal as-

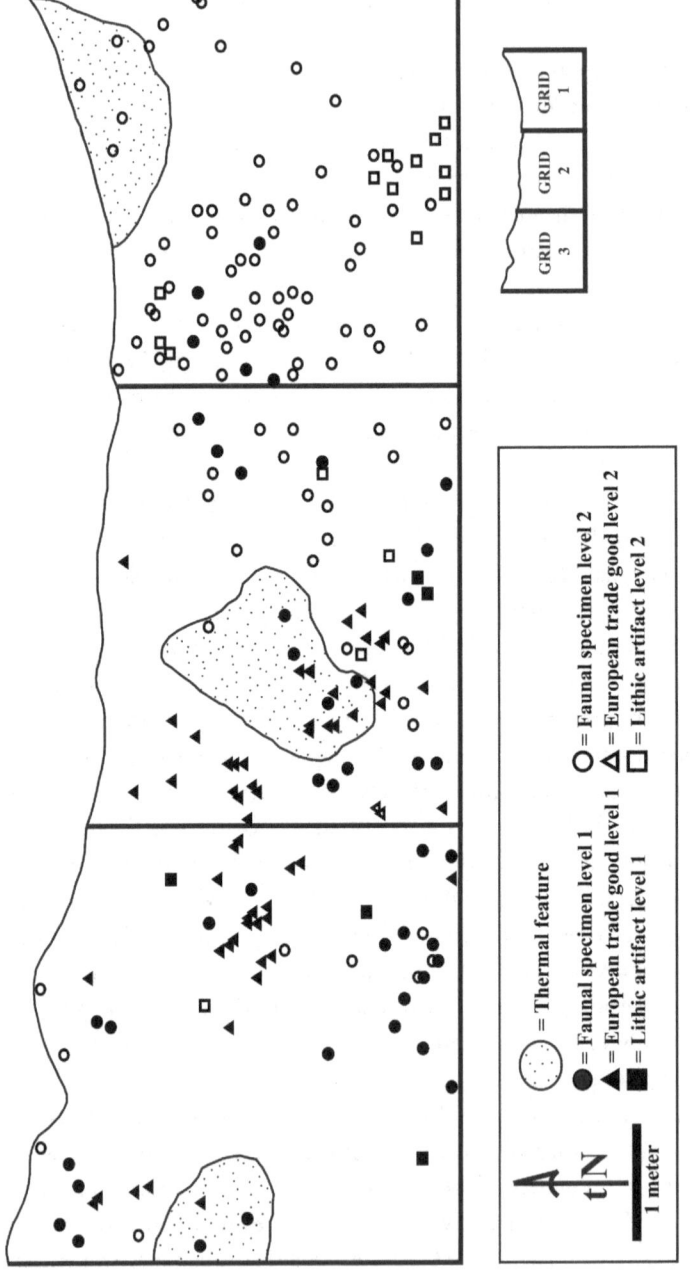

4.2. Lykins Valley site excavation block

semblage was likely deposited at the same time. Given these multiple lines of supporting evidence, it is reasonable to analyze the entire post-contact assemblage as a single entity.

The lithic assemblage suggests that limited tool production took place on-site and tools brought to the site were used and maintained. Of the 621 total lithic artifacts, 498 are retouched flakes and only 10 are formal tools. Although 89.2 percent of the assemblage is made from raw materials found within 10 kilometers of the site, all of the formal tools appear to be manufactured from nonlocal tool stone. Two pieces of obsidian debitage found at the site source to the Jemez Mountains in the Santa Fe region of north-central New Mexico (Newton 2008:65). The Jemez Mountain sources are common in late-period contexts throughout the Southwest and east of the Rocky Mountains (Shackley 2005), and suggest links between the Lykins Valley group and groups to the southwest.

Three arrow points and two grooved abraders indicate the use of bow and arrow technology, despite the possession of firearms. Two of the arrow points are trinotched, a type found throughout the region in post-contact contexts, and the groove widths of the abraders are well within the range of deviation found in Thomas's (1978) sample of ethnographic and archaeological arrow shaft widths. The presence of these artifacts is not surprising given that early trade muskets were of poor quality and Indian hunters were generally unable to obtain gunpowder and lead in the quantities necessary for hunting. Even with adequate supplies, the bow and arrow was a much better weapon when hunting on horseback, and Indian hunters rarely used firearms for this purpose before the 1860s (Ray 1974).

The use of local lithic sources, probably secondary cobbles found in alluvial deposits near the site, meant procurement was likely embedded in other daily subsistence activities (Newton 2008:74). These factors, along with acquisition of trade items, may indicate that site occupants were less reliant on lithic technology than a pre-contact group would have been. The lack of formal tools and structured reductive strategies indicates an informal use of indigenous technology, although the presence of tools such as arrow points and endscrapers (n = 5) indicate it was still important to their economy. The presence of ground stone and endscrapers attests to the varied activities taking place at the site, characteristic of a long-term occupation.

Faunal analysis of the post-contact component indicates that at least three bison *(Bison bison)*, three mule deer *(Odocoileus hemionus)*, and one pronghorn *(Antilocapra americana)* were consumed at the site between late summer or fall and midwinter (Newton 2008:158). Two elements identified as horse *(Equus caballus)* were recovered as well but they are excluded from any discussion of food resources given the small number of specimens and their predominate use by post-contact Indian groups as beasts of burden. A comparison between the skeletal portion (i.e., axial, cranial, forelimb, hindlimb) frequencies of the bison, mule deer, and pronghorn with the frequencies expected from a complete generalized ungulate skeleton demonstrates that all skeletal portions are well represented in the assemblage. This suggests these animals were brought to the site as relatively complete carcasses. The majority of these animals (six of the seven) had live weights of less than 100 kilograms, which would have made the equestrian transport of whole carcasses possible. The Shannon Evenness Index, used to quantify the type of transport strategy at the site, indicates that the bison ($E = 0.915$) and the same size class mule deer/pronghorn ($E = 0.883$) compare most favorably with a bulk ($E = 0.980$) or unbiased ($E = 0.842$) strategy, also suggesting the use of the horse (using method and comparative values from Faith and Gordon 2007).

Once at camp, the carcasses were intensively processed as indicated by extensive bone fragmentation, impact flakes, and cones. There are 1,317 specimens (85.9 percent) that exhibit green bone break and, of these, fragments less than 5 centimeters in maximum length compose 50.5 percent of the total assemblage. There were 68 impact cones recorded, mainly on bison long bones, and the assemblage also contained 124 impact flakes. The presence of impact flakes is evidence of in situ processing.

The faunal remains also provide information on seasonality. The eruption of the first molar, identical on two juvenile bison mandibles in the assemblage, provides an age of four to five months at the time of death. The assemblage also contains a mule deer frontal exhibiting a partially disintegrating pedicle indicating the antler is about to be shed. Bison, being a birth pulse species, generally calve in April or May and mule deer generally shed their antlers in January, placing the site occupation from late summer (August or September) into winter. The length of occupation and processing intensity support a scenario where carcasses were being brought individually into the camp and completely processed for meat and marrow before more animals were procured. This is logical in an overwintering occupation where snow and inclement weather would have made hunting difficult, necessitating exhausting all available resources before hunting again. The lack of carnivore modification on the faunal remains likely results from the site occupants exhausting all available bone nutrients and/or remaining in proximity to the discarded bones, limiting carnivore access.

As mentioned previously, the faunal assemblage includes two specimens identified as horse (a distal metapodial and a proximal scapula). Based on differences in ^{13}C isotopic ratios of the two specimens these two elements may well represent different animals (see Table 4.3). The carbon isotopic signature from the horse metapodial is indicative of an animal foraging north of the site area, whereas the signature from the scapula indicates an animal from the region. This is based on comparison to a sample of ^{13}C isotopic signatures (horse and bison) from 193 bone collagen assays from over 50 sites throughout the Great Plains dating to within the last 2,000 years (from Boutton et al. 1991; Bozell et al. 1997; Byerly and Meltzer

2005; Chisholm et al. 1986; Huebner and Boutton 1994; Meltzer 2006; Tieszen et al. 1997; Tuross and Fogel 1994). The sample from the Lykins Valley site shows a significant correlation ($r = -0.386$, $p < 0.01$) between latitude and ^{13}C isotopic signature; a regression equation derived from the sample places the isotopic signature from the horse metapodial in the northern Great Plains, significantly north of Lykins Valley. This is a generalized comparison at this point and warrants further investigation; however, other artifacts from the site substantiate ties to the north and/or northeast.

A single English flake-type gunflint found at the site provides further evidence of northern trade inputs and gives a *terminus post quem* for the post-contact occupation. This gunflint has diagnostic impact cones, or demicones, that are the by-product of a manufacturing technique developed by the British around 1780 (Witthoft 1966:36). Fort Michilimackinac, abandoned by the British in 1781, contains no English flake gunflints of this type (despite hundreds of recovered gunflints) because they had yet to appear in North America (Hamilton and Emery 1988:244). The portions of at least one and possibly two Type A Variety II brass kettle lugs (based on the Brain [1979] classification system) were recovered. Kettles of this type found at the 18th-century Trudeau and Gilbert sites (in Louisiana and Texas, respectively) indicate they are of French origin. Type A Variety II kettles have also been found in association with English artifacts (Wheeler et al. 1975:63–64). At Fort Michilimackinac, occupied by both the French and British between 1715 and 1781, French-made kettles were commonly used by both nations (Stone 1974:175). These artifacts reflect French and English trade influence on the plains during the 18th and early 19th century (Hämäläinen 1998; Wishart 1979).

Glass beads, in historic archaeological contexts, are found throughout the Great Plains; their trade to and use by Indian groups were widespread. The dimensional data for Type IIa beads (based on the Kidd and Kidd [1970] classification system) from Lykins Valley cannot be differentiated statistically (using t-tests) in measurements of outer diameter, inner diameter, and length from a northern Wyoming bead sample (Scheiber 1994) that was relatively dated to circa 1810. The Lykins Valley beads are larger and more variable in size than several mid- to late-19th-century bead assemblages. Coupled with the lack of red beads in the assemblage, these data point to a late-18th- or early-19th-century date.

Evidence from another site in the Lykins Valley provides possible group affiliation. A rock art site (5LR293), located on Boxelder Creek 3 kilometers upstream from the Lykins Valley site, cannot be definitively associated with the occupation at the latter, but its characteristics suggest contemporaneity, providing ancillary evidence as to the possible tribal affiliation of the Lykins Valley site occupants. A petroglyph panel at the site, based on stylistic attributes, is from the Biographic Tradition (early 18th century to late 19th century) as defined by Keyser and Klassen (2001). It depicts a figure seated in a saddle with a high pommel and cantle on

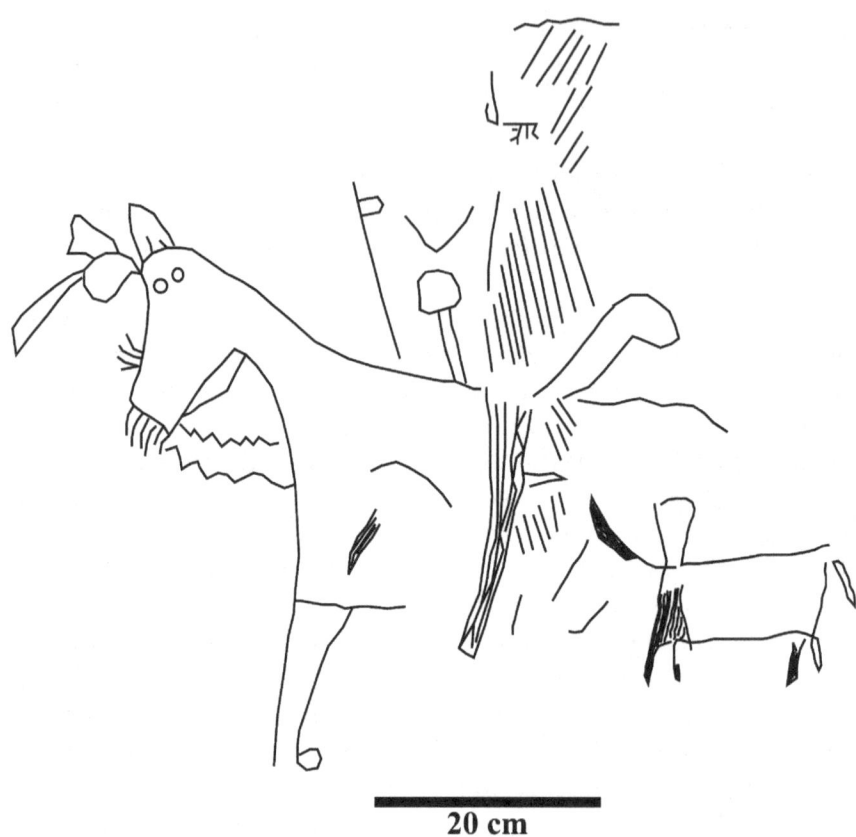

4.3. Rock art panel from 5LR293 based on image in Morris et al. (1979:89)

a horse wearing a Spanish chain bit (see Figure 4.3). The Spanish chain bit was first documented on the northwestern Great Plains by the La Vérendrye expedition in 1739 (Smith 1980:100). The saddle and bit characteristics and overall style match that from Cheyenne ledger drawings (cf. Keyser 1987), indicating a possible Cheyenne affiliation. However, the zigzag reins on the figure have been attributed to Comanche artists at other sites (Loendorf and Olsen 2003). Either interpretation indicates a Southern Plains influence that is different from the northern influence demonstrated by the trade goods.

Conclusion

The overall indication based on the assemblage at the Lykins Valley site, along with the other post-contact evidence is that, despite acquisition of items of European manufacture, the occupants of this region were largely unaffected by European markets. It was not until the development of the fur trade in the area that an influential market economy was established. In general, the pattern indicates that the occupants of Lykins Valley were able to acquire numerous trade items (e.g., guns and kettles) without becoming dependent on fur or hide production. The Lykins Valley site is a snapshot of the period in which Indian groups on the periphery of the market economy were able to take advantage of trade opportunities and garner new technologies (including the horse), yet still largely employed indigenous modes of subsistence.

The west-central Great Plains during the late 18th and early 19th centuries was a place of little or no European presence and largely pre-contact indigenous lifeways. Trade in French and English goods from the Middle Missouri (through middlemen, or in down-the-line trade) and southern items (e.g., obsidian, Spanish chain bits) from the Comanche trading centers on the Arkansas would have been accessible from this region. Classic studies of trade by Jablow (1950) and Wishart (1979) demonstrate the dual influences of trade from the north and south into the central plains. Indications of north and south trade, combined with rock art imagery at 5LR293 make a strong case for Cheyenne occupation of the Lykins Valley. The Cheyenne were in the region when the site was occupied and were well connected to trade networks (Jablow 1950).

Some evidence at the site, such as the small group size and winter hunting, may indicate some group upheaval or dislocation, but it is reasonable given the trade-goods evidence that the group was taking advantage of an ecological niche where game was readily available year round. There is no evidence to suggest that Indian group identity was compromised at this time. In fact, most of the evidence is suggestive of an autonomous group that was occupying an area rich in natural resources with access to trade from both the north/northeast and south. Indigenous artifacts at the site indicate that, despite the introduction of European technologies, it was "business as usual" in Lykins Valley and the Indian inhabitants took advantage of the location on multiple levels. They could access or be involved in both the southern and northern trade networks while living in a location that had a great abundance of natural resources and had not yet been impinged upon by Europeans.

5 / Negotiating Borders
The Southern Caddo and Their Relationships with Colonial Governments in East Texas
P. Shawn Marceaux and Timothy K. Perttula

Introduction

Caddo groups inhabited areas covering parts of modern Texas, Louisiana, Oklahoma, and Arkansas for at least eight hundred years before the first but intermittent European contacts that took place in circa A.D. 1542 (see Hudson 1997:353–379). A variety of written accounts from the time of sustained contact, more than 140 years later, along with archaeological investigations beginning in the early 20th century, have informed and influenced our understanding of the social, political, and economic organization of the Caddo peoples. It is known from those historic accounts that the southern Caddo were organized into three loosely affiliated groups, probably kin related: "the Hasinai groups lived in the Neches and Angelina River Valleys in east Texas, the Kadohadacho groups on the Red River in the Great Bend area, and the Natchitoches groups on the Red River in the vicinity of the French post of Natchitoches established in 1714" (Perttula 1992:16) (see Figure 5.1).

In this chapter, we first provide a historical sketch of Caddo and colonial relationships, based primarily on trade, but always imbued with underlying political and social machinations of both the Caddo people and the various colonial governments (cf. Barr 2005, 2007; Smith 2005) in east Texas from circa 1775 to the middle of the 19th century, the temporal focus of this volume. Following a review of the archaeological record for this period, which is unfortunately still not very well known, we turn to pertinent historical research on the Caddo peoples (Carter 1995; Lee 1998; Smith 1991, 1995, 2005) and original documents (Bolton 1914; Jackson 2000, 2003; Kinnaird 1949), such as administrative correspondences, declarations, directives, and official inspection diaries. These documents illuminate the course and character of the different Caddo groups during this period of expand-

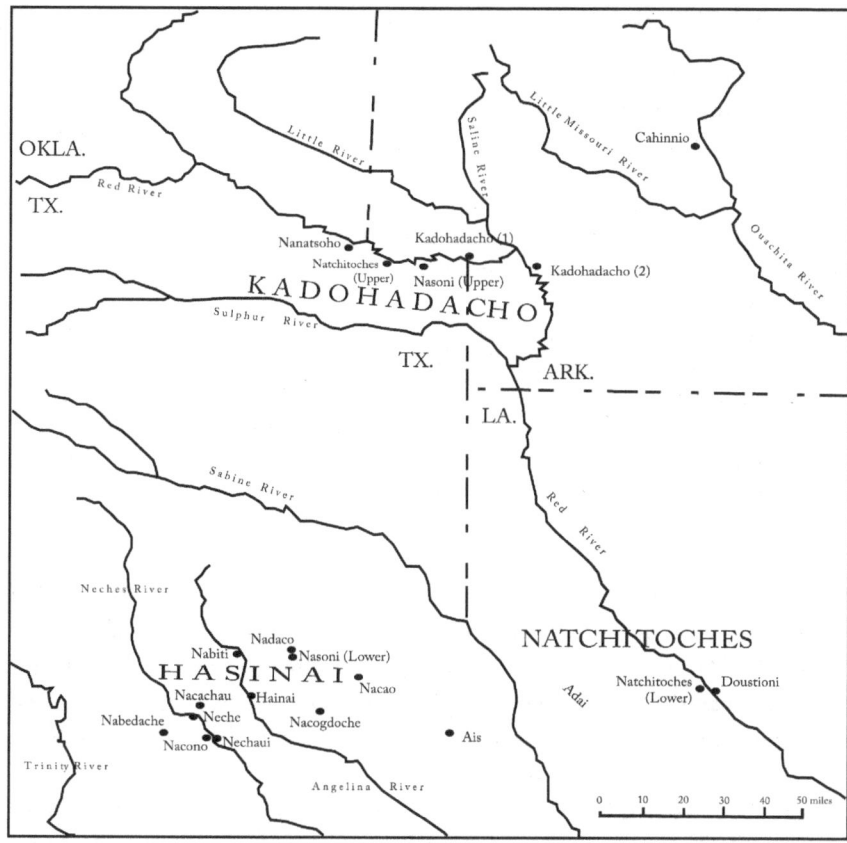

5.1. The distribution of Hasinai, Kadohadacho, and Natchitoches groups and other related tribes

ing market economies. The scarcity of archaeological sites identified from the area dating to this period makes it difficult to contextualize, but along with our discussion of Indian-colonial economies, we attempt to elucidate how Caddo groups in east Texas maintained cultural identities while adapting to the changing political and economic landscape, especially the land-grabbing proclivities of European Americans after the first decade of the 19th century (Smith 2005:96).

A Historical Sketch

Less than a decade after the first permanent European settlement within the present boundary of Texas (Chipman 1992), missions San Francisco de los Tejas and El Santísimo Nombre de María (1690) were founded among Caddo groups near the Neches River in east Texas (see Table 5.1 and Figure 5.1). The early missions in east Texas (which lasted until 1693) were established to block both the real and

5.1. Historical context and events in Caddo and colonial history

French and Indian War	1754–1763
Treaty of Paris, ends the French and Indian War	1763
Marqués de Rubí inspection of Texas missions	1767
Spanish flag formally raised in Louisiana	1769
All Spanish missions abandoned in provinces of Texas and Louisiana	1772
Treaty of Paris, formally ends American Revolutionary War	1783
The trading house of Barr and Davenport founded in Nacogdoches	1798
French reacquire Louisiana	1800
Louisiana purchased by the United States	1803
Freeman and Custis Red River expedition and the Neutral Ground Agreement	1806
U.S. declares war on Great Britain	1812
Adam-Onís Treaty, settled boundary and possession of Louisiana and Texas	1819
Caddo sign cession of Red River homeland	1835
Caddo removed to Indian Territory	1859

perceived threat of French encroachment and to attempt to Christianize the Caddo peoples. However, the difficulty of supplying these frontier posts, reestablished in 1716 and 1721, the Caddo rejection of and indifference to the bumbling and ill-conceived Spanish missionizing and diplomatic efforts (Barr 2004, 2005), as well as changing international politics led to the abandonment of the missions in fewer than 80 years (Barr 2007; Carlson 1996).

With the end of the French and Indian War (1754–63) and the Treaty of Paris, France ceded the territory of Louisiana to Spain and east Texas became an interior province—at least as far as the colonial Spanish government was concerned. For the Caddo, these east Texas lands were their sacred homelands and had always been viewed that way: "the Spanish presence in 'Texas' often had little relevance to the region's predominant native political and economic relations" (Barr 2005:150).

Spain, aware that Louisiana was never financially profitable, still sought to deter British expansionism (Chipman 1992). However, Spain's initial inability to govern in Louisiana led them to leave the administration largely in the hands of French agents. According to Bolton (1914:72), the decision to carry on the French system of annual presents and a network of French and Creole traders was the "line of least resistance," and after a few years the system extended to include the Caddo tribes of Texas. The Caddo were already known to the French and Spanish as active traders, eager to obtain material goods. As Gregory et al. (2004:65) stated, "Caddo Indians viewed the Spanish more as a source for material goods rather than spiritual edification."

The exact date of the introduction and scope of infectious epidemic diseases among the Caddo people is uncertain (Derrick and Wilson 2001), but late-18th-century correspondence documents their devastating effect. For example, an epidemic in 1777 struck Hasinai groups in east Texas particularly hard. Bigotes, chief of the Hainai; Gorgoritos, chief of the Bidai (an Atakapan-speaking tribe); and a Nabedache chief all died (Bolton 1914; Carter 1995; Kinnaird 1949). A decade later a "cruel fever" took the lives of two-thirds of the Caddo, along with many Europeans (Derrick and Wilson 2001:94; Smith 1991). The influx of other American Indian groups, displaced and pushed westward, and Osage attacks were also a constant concern. After 1795, the Kadohadacho moved south from the Red River homeland of their ancestors, coalescing as a means of survival. The consolidated Caddo tribes renamed their new home on Caddo Lake *Sha'chahdínnih* after the first village of all Caddo peoples noted in origin stories (Carter 1995:217; Parsons et al. 2002).

After the United States war for independence in 1783, the area east of the Mississippi River came under its control. West of the Mississippi, jurisdictional differences made administration complicated for the Spanish. Secret dealings transferred the territory of Louisiana back to the French in 1800, only to have it purchased by the United States in 1803. While the United States thought the purchase included part of the Texas territory, the Spanish did not agree. Once again the Caddo found themselves on the border of rival colonial governments. The ambiguous nature of the boundary, exemplified by the 1806 Neutral Ground agreement (Haggard 1942, 1945), serves as a metaphor for Caddo and European American political and economic relations.

Jurisdiction of the Caddo lands was contested by the Spanish and Americans. Hasinai groups were clearly living in Spanish Texas, but the place and affiliation of the Kadohadacho was less clear, at least to the European and American governments. To the Kadohadacho their place on the land was unambiguous. As tension between the United States and Spain increased, the Caddo remained neutral until Dehahuit, the Kadohadacho chief, gave a telling speech to Governor Claiborne (*Mississippi Messenger* 1806). Carter (1995:238) states that "with these words the Grand Caddo declared the transfer of his people's loyalty—not their land—to the Americans."

By around 1834 the American population in Texas had reached 20,000—about 3,500 of which lived in the Department of Nacogdoches (Jackson 2003:253), and 700 in the community of Nacogdoches (Sanchez 1926:283)—while Indian peoples comprised only an estimated 14,200 individuals (see Schoolcraft 1851–57). Most of this population was from recently arrived immigrant Indian groups such as the Cherokee, Choctaw, Kickapoo, Shawnee, Delaware, and Alabama-Coushatta. This marked the first time since the European colonization and settlement of the near Southwest that non-Indians made up the majority of the population living in east Texas (Carter 1995:275–276). The total Caddo population at that time was fewer than 2,000 individuals (see Table 5.2).

In 1835, the Caddo signed a cession with the United States, transferring ap-

5.2. Caddo populations through the colonial era

Year	Source	Warriors[a]	Population
Hasinai			
1699	Pierre Talon	600–700	2,400–2,800
1716	Ramon		4,000–5,000
1721	Aguayo		ca. 1,378
1779	De Mezieres	135	540
1783	Morfi	380 (?)	1,520
1805	Sibley	200	800
1818–1820	*Cincinnati Gazette*	150	650
1820	Padilla		1,450
1828	Terán	23	92
1828	Berlandier	30–40	120–160
1834	Almonte		400
1836	Republic of Texas		200[b]
1847	Burnet	200	800
1851	Stem	ca. 100	ca. 315
Hainai			
1783	Morfi	80	320
1798	Davenport	60	240
1809	Salcedo	60	240
1828	Berlandier	10	40
Nabedache			
1779	De Mezieres	40	160
1783	Morfi	40	160
1798	Davenport	80	320
1819	Padilla		500
1828	Terán	15	60
1828	Berlandier	80	400
Nacogdoche			
1783	Morfi	300	1,200
1798	Davenport	50[c]	200
1809	Salcedo	50	200
1828	Berlandier	50	200
Nadaco			
1798	Davenport	100	400
1809	Salcedo	100	100
1828	Terán/Sanchez	29	116
1828	Berlandier	30	150
1856	Neighbors	38	190

Year	Source	Warriors[a]	Population
1856	Neighbors		235
Ais			
1716	French traders		320
1779	De Mezieres	20	80
1805	Sibley		25
1818–20	*Cincinnati Gazette*		50
1820	Padilla		300
1828	Muckleroy/Terán		640
1828	Berlandier		300
Kadohadacho			
1700	Bienville	500–600	2,000–2,400
1709	La Harpe		2,500
1718	Bienville	200	800
1719	La Harpe		400
1773	De Mezieres	160	640
1798	Davenport	200	800
1805	Sibley	100	400
1809	Salcedo	200	800
1818	*Cincinnati Gazette*	120	500–600
1820	Miller	300	1,200
1820	Padilla		2,000
1825	Schoolcraft		450
1828	Berlandier	300	1,200
1829	Porter		450
1834	Almonte		500
1836	Morfit	150	1,000
1838	Riley	120–130	480–520
1838	Office of Indian Affairs		156[d]
1849	Neighbors	280	1,400[e]
1851	Stem		161[f]
1851	Upshaw		167[g]
1854	Hill		500[h]
1856	Neighbors	35	175
1857	Neighbors		235
1859	Neighbors		244
Natchitoches			
1700	Bienville	450	1,800
1718	Bienville	80	320

Continued on the next page

5.2 *Continued*

Year	Source	Warriors[a]	Population
1719	La Harpe		200
1805	Sibley	12	48
1825	Gray	10	40
1825	Schoolcraft		61
Yatasi			
1773	De Mezieres	3	12
1798	Davenport	40[i]	160
1805	Sibley	8	32
1809	Salcedo	30	120
1825	Gray	12	48

[a] One warrior is assumed to equate to four members of a family, but it is likely that this underestimates population sizes; some sources estimated five members to a family or five people per warrior. This table is based in part on the work of Swanton (1942:22–23) and Jelks (2002:5–6).
[b] Hasinai and Nacogdoche
[c] Nacogdoche and Ais groups
[d] Shreveport Kadohadacho
[e] Kadohadacho, Hainai, and Nadaco
[f] Texas Kadohadacho only
[g] Oklahoma Kadohadacho only
[h] Kadohadacho, Hainai, and Nadaco
[i] Yatasi and Adaes groups

proximately one million acres, which "cut away their Red River heartland" in return for an agreed-upon price (Carter 1995:273). The United States was supposed to pay the Caddo $30,000 in goods and horses immediately and $10,000 in cash every year for the next five years, and the Caddo were expected to leave the territory and move into the Mexican province in July 1836.

In October of that year, the Texans' revolt against Mexico began, and the threat of Caddo groups allying with the Mexicans prompted the Americans to ask the Caddo to stay. Representatives of Texas signed a declaration guaranteeing to Indians "peaceable enjoyment of their rights to their lands" (Carter 1995:276), but in 1838 Mirabeau Lamar (the second president of the Republic of Texas) instituted a policy of complete removal (Neighbours 1973). Even in October 1838, when a group of Caddo had been brought by the United States government to live temporarily on an island on the Red River near Shreveport, Louisiana (since they had no permanent home in Texas), the Republic of Texas sent a force to confront and disarm the Caddo. This action was based on an unproven presumption by the Texans that the Caddo's "perfidious actions present a continuous catalogue of depredations on the most exposed and defenseless settlements of the country" (Jackson 2005:265). The Texans outnumbered the Caddo more than 10 to 1.

Between 1836 and 1842, the Hasinai, Nadaco, and Kadohadacho tribes were being forcibly pushed out of east Texas (Perttula and Nelson 2006:20). From 1846, when Texas was annexed to the United States, to their removal to Indian Territory in 1859, the lives of Caddo peoples were fraught with violence (see Anderson 2005; Moore 2006, 2007), constant relocation, and uncertainty. The Caddo's precipitous removal from the Brazos Reserve (1854–59) was led by Major Robert Neighbors, a proven friend and ally of the Caddo people (Neighbours 1975).

The Frontier Market Economy: Caddo and Colonial Economies in East Texas, circa 1775–1838

Over two hundred years after initial contact, the Caddo were undoubtedly familiar with the requisite social, legal, and religious principles of colonial governments. Material trade and exchange, not always congruent with those principles, was a vital objective of people living on the frontier. Trade was negotiated through alliances, fictive and kin relations, and intermarriage (see Barr 2007; Lee 1998). Propelled into the colonial economy, the Caddo provided peltries, furs, livestock, and surplus food supplies in return for muskets, powder, knives, pots, clothing, and beads. In fact, the peltry, horse, gun, bear fat, and salt trades carried on by the Caddo in the frontier market economy was part of a broad exchange network composed of Europeans and aboriginal peoples that reflected basic and pervasive political and economic alliances. At least for a time, these economic relationships were based "for the most part, on cooperation, accommodation, and mutual support" (Gregory et al. 2004:65). Until the early 1810s (see Flores 1985:93; Smith 2005:96–119), there were strong economic ties between the Spanish, French (and French Creoles), and Caddo peoples.

By the late 18th century, with the Spanish acquisition of Louisiana and the removal of its settlers and missions, Spanish priorities and policies had changed; their only colonial threat was the United States. As a result, supplies and gifts to the Caddo of east Texas may have diminished, at least officially, after the mid-1780s. Juan María Vicencio de Ripperdá, the governor of Texas from 1770 to 1778, requested the power to license traders, even those from Louisiana, but his petition was denied (Bolton 1914:79). A letter from Gil Ybarbo (1780) in Nacogdoches petitioned for the return of a licensed French trader who had moved to Natchitoches. Hasinai Caddo groups were requesting, as promised, "an annual present, a trader in every village, and a table of prices for every chief in which would be shown the price that he should pay the trader for his goods and the trader should give for his skins" (Kinnaird 1949:II:390).

Between 1777 and 1785, however, gifts to the aboriginal populations comprised between 10–40 percent of the expenses of the Spanish province of Louisiana (Perttula 1992:Table 22). We also suspect that illicit and unreported trade activities of Louisiana Frenchmen and mestizos continued unabated along the frontier (see Usner

1992, 1998). Lieutenant Governor Athanase de Meziere, because of the confidence he was held in by the Caddo, was also able to foster mutual trade relationships as well as Spanish diplomatic efforts (Bolton 1914:80–84; Perttula et al. 2008:88). These annual presents were a reflection of political and economic commitments of friendship and alliances between the Caddo peoples and Europeans. The annual presents were substantial to all the Indian groups living in the province of Louisiana, accounting for 30–40 percent of the total expenses of the province in the 1780s alone (Perttula 1994:Figure 3; Usner 1992:Table 7). Among the goods provided as presents to the Caddo, the most important (at least in terms of their value in pesos) were gunpowder, muskets or fusils, musket balls, cloth, shirts, glass beads, hatchets, axes, and blankets.

The Caddo threatened that if these were not provided within the next four months, the Spanish would be considered enemies. Still, in 1783, a letter from Governor Domingo Cabello ordered those in Natchitoches to refrain from giving the Texas Yatasi, Hasinai, Ais, and Nacogdoches any trade goods (Kinnaird 1949:III). The justification was to keep goods from flowing into the hands of the hostile Lipan Apaches.

The situation in east Texas was somewhat improved by the House of Barr and Davenport (1798–1812), headquartered in Nacogdoches; this became a new trade distribution center. Generally, this commercial house shipped in merchandise from Louisiana for sale in Texas, and peltries, furs, and livestock were transported back to Louisiana (Haggard 1945). Barr and Davenport were allowed to trade out of territorial and economic necessity. Returning Spanish troops needed supplies and the commercial house afforded a way to secure presents and distribute goods to Indian groups such as the Caddo. Agents of Barr and Davenport were granted a monopoly on all Indian trade, but had to continually ask permission to send horses and livestock to Louisiana and west Florida. Permission for obtaining merchandise from New Orleans was "a temporary privilege and . . . applicable only to the articles secured for the Indian trade" (Haggard 1945:74).

In 1805, Dr. John Sibley was assigned as Indian agent by the Secretary of War Henry Dearborn for the Louisiana area and the United States established a permanent Indian trading factory at Natchitoches (Smith 1991). As Perttula et al. note (2008:89): "Unlike Spain, the United States did not by policy appoint French Creoles to important positions in the territorial government, but Sibley sought them out to learn about reciprocity, gift-giving, and the use of fictive kinship in cementing alliances." The American approach of establishing a centralized Office of Indian Affairs, with agents such as Sibley, to coordinate the trading efforts of factories that supplied Indian groups across the nation, proved to be more successful than the Spanish monopoly of Barr and Davenport, with a few individual traders and trappers bound by numerous trade restrictions, and a general prohibition of trade with Louisiana. The U.S. trade factories on the Red River came to dominate the market economy, underdeveloped as it was on the Caddo Texas/Louisiana frontier, with respect to the consumer goods that moved through it or the products that supported it. In 1818 and 1819, for example, more than $5,000 worth of trade business was carried out with Indians at the Sulphur Fork Factory (Perttula 1994:87 n. 3). Jean Louis Berlandier observed in 1828 that the Kadohadacho now cultivated "very little land," followed the migrations of the buffalo herds, and did a "thriving trade in furs," which were exchanged in Natchitoches and other U.S. government trading factories (Ewers 1969:107).

Caddo Archaeology, 1775–1850

The Caddo archaeological record in east Texas from circa 1775 to 1850 is very poorly documented, which is remarkable considering the relatively widespread distribution of Historic Caddo sites dating from the late 17th through the mid 18th centuries (see Figure 5.2). The Caddo tradition, the westernmost American Indian society affiliated in a broad way with their Mississippian neighbors, is recognizable archaeologically from its beginnings circa A.D. 800–900. The Caddo were maize agriculturists (or at least had been since ca. A.D. 1300) and lived in permanent but dispersed communities, including several large villages. They made distinctive and beautifully crafted ceramics that were used for cooking, food storage, and food serving, were long-distance traders of exotic and prestige goods, and constructed monumental architecture at a series of centrally placed mound centers along major streams, aboriginal trails, and river crossings. Many earlier Historic Caddo sites (i.e., those predating ca. 1720) contain few European trade goods, and domestic remains found in archaeological contexts consist primarily of decorated and plain ceramic fine wares and utility wares, triangular and stemmed arrow points, ceramic pipes, ground stone, and bone tools (Perttula 1992; Story 1995).

Using the distinctive Caddo ceramics of the era and the presence of European trade goods, including glass beads, guns, gun parts, and metal in archaeological contexts, over one hundred historic Caddo sites are currently known in east Texas (Marceaux 2007; Perttula and Middlebrook 2007). Most of these have been found in either the Allen phase (ca. 1650–1830) area of east Texas, in the Natchitoches, Louisiana, area (see Figure 5.1), or along the Red River in the Great Bend area visited by the Freeman-Custis expedition in 1806 (Flores 1984). Some of these villages were large and would have been impressive to behold. Freeman and Custis described the principal Caddo village on the Red River (see Figure 5.2), abandoned in 1788, as follows: "Around and near to this pond [on the Red River], are to be seen the vestiges of the Caddo habitations; it was the largest of their villages, and their cultivated fields extended for five or six miles from it in every direction" (Flores 1984:188).

One of the more important sites of the circa 1775–1850 period is the Timber

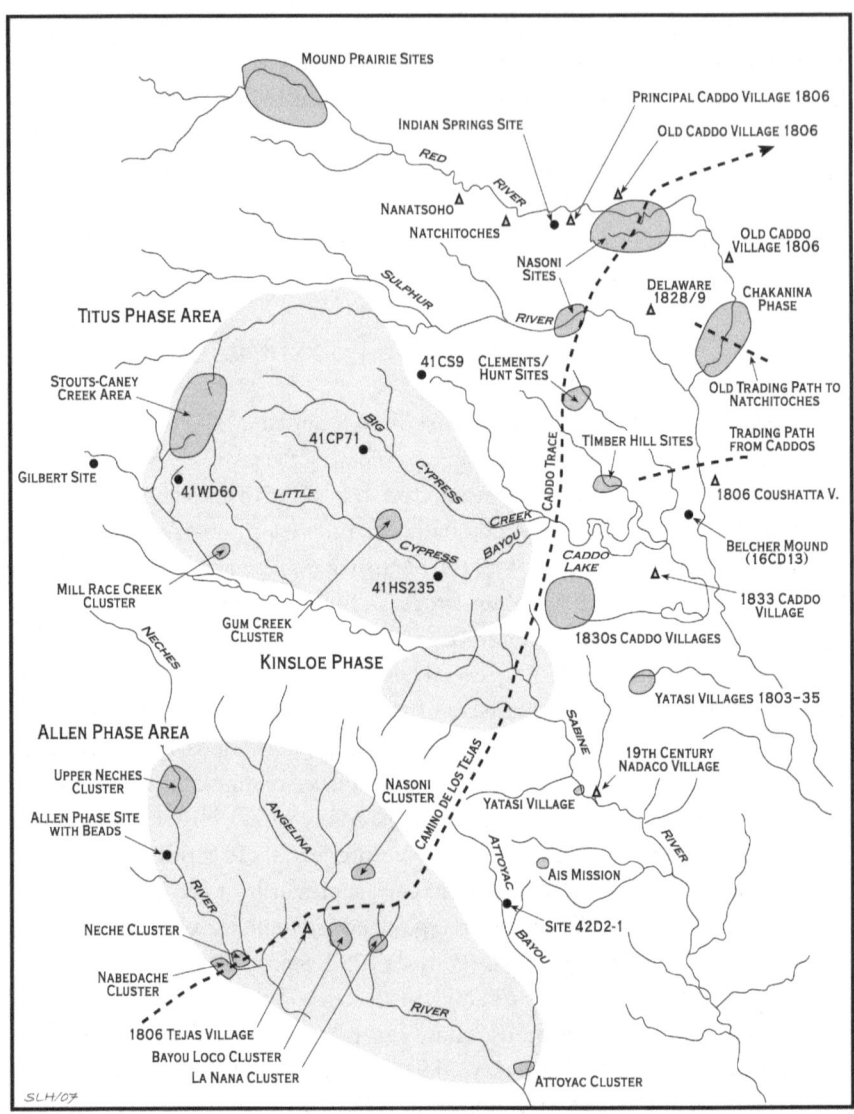

5.2. Historic Caddo archaeological sites and phases in east Texas

Hill site (41MR211), or *Sha'chahdínnih*. It has been characterized by some as the "last village of the Kadohadacho Caddo in the Caddo homeland region" (Parsons et al. 2002:iii), although there were at least four other Kadohadacho villages in east Texas up to the fall of 1838 (see Tiller 2007, 2008). Timber Hill was the principal Kadohadacho village in the early 19th century and was probably occupied until the early 1830s (Tiller 2007, 2008). It was named after the first village founded after the Caddo emerged from the earth and left *Cha'kani'na*, the place of crying (Carter

1995:217; Dorsey 1905:7–13; Swanton 1942:27–28). The site was established on Caddo Lake in 1800 (Parsons et al. 2002:5), likely covered several hundred acres, perhaps 0.5 miles in diameter, and had at least three hundred families living there during much of its existence (see Table 5.2).

The Caddo ceramic tradition continued unabated at the Timber Hill site, even at this late date (Parsons et al. 2002:35), as did traditional culinary practices of the Caddo people. It appears that the ceramics at Timber Hill were made and used for cooking, re-heating, serving, and storage of food stuffs, and probably had the same range in vessel form and size as did earlier Caddo ceramic assemblages. Even after extensive contact with Europeans, presumably more than a century after the introduction of metal cookware (i.e., iron kettles), the Caddo continued to use their traditional ceramics. This strongly implies that traditional means of food processing and culinary practices were maintained by the Caddo living at Timber Hill and that they held fast to their cultural and social traditions.

The corn grown and eaten at Timber Hill consisted of traditional varieties, as well as a larger variety of Eastern Complex corn, but "both kinds of corn described by eighteenth-century Spanish missionaries were simultaneously cultivated into the nineteenth century" (Parsons et al. 2002:86). Features found on the site suggest that deer hides were carefully smoked over smudge pits to produce high-quality deerskins.

The Caddo ceramics found at the Timber Hill site are an apparent amalgamation of the traditions of different but ethnically related Kadohadacho groups because they are diverse in terms of tempers used in the vessel paste (i.e., shell temper favored by some Caddo groups, and grog and bone by others), and in the range of decorations seen on the fine and utility wares. In another example of Caddo ceramic manufacture and culinary continuity, several mid-1830s Caddo vessels apparently collected from Caddo peoples living in northwestern Louisiana are similar in vessel shape to late-18th-century vessel forms and have recognizable Historic Caddo engraved motifs (Perttula 2001).

European goods, including ceramic cups, bowls, and plates, glass bottles, metal containers such as kettles (an important item offered by trading factories, and employed by the Caddo to render bear fat) and Dutch ovens, as well as various domestic tools, had become part of the material culture of the Caddo living at Timber Hill, and many began to supplement or even replace goods of Caddo manufacture by this time (Parsons et al. 2002; Perttula et al. 2008). In addition to these more common European goods obtained in trade from U.S. factories, there were glass beads, military buttons from traded greatcoats, thimbles, tinklers, hawk bells, gun parts, horse trappings (harness buckles and rings and a bridle bit), and nails from crates or wagons. Clearly, throughout the first quarter of the 19th century, the Caddo participated in the frontier market economy and benefited materially from it.

Another important, but little known, Caddo site occupied in the first years of the 19th century is the Middle Caddo village in east Texas. This is one of a number of Caddo villages probably established along the ambiguous boundary between American Louisiana and Texas after the 1835 U.S. treaty with the Caddo. As an 1837 petition from the Caddo to the U.S. government indicates, they purposefully established their villages outside the domain of the United States:

> We have established our villages near the head of Lake Sodo [Caddo Lake] which we believe to be without the boundary of the United States, but on running the line between Mexico and the U.S. should it be found to be within the jurisdiction of the latter, we will instantly remove further to the west [into Texas]. Hope you will inform the President of our great wish to have this line run out as we can make no permanent settlement until this is done. [Caddo Chiefs 1837]

The Middle Caddo village was still in existence in early 1838 (Oates 1963:26; Tiller 2007). This village (41HS840) appears to cover about forty acres, based on very limited investigations, which primarily included shovel testing and metal detecting. Items obtained in the market economy abound, and include such trade goods obtained from nearby U.S. trade factories as gun parts and musket balls (of several calibers), gunflints, axe blades, iron kettles, case knives, horse gear, pearlware cups and plates, and wine bottle glass. There is evidence here of both blacksmithing and the on-site manufacture of rifle balls, and there are pieces or cutouts of silver ornaments and copper sheet fragments that suggest the Caddo were manufacturing ornamental items from available trade metal sources. They also made sheet copper and iron arrow points. One of the square cut nails had evidence of use as a tool, as did pieces of chipped glass; chipped glass and ceramics were probably used as scrapers on deer hides, and such implements have been recovered from other circa 1790–1835 Caddo sites (McCrocklin 1993). Caddo ceramic sherds from vessels and pipes are also present at the site.

The wide range of metal artifacts from both Timber Hill and the Middle Caddo Village indicates that the Caddo living there had ready access to European and American goods. In some cases the metal goods were used and reworked by the Caddo to suit their own purposes. When the metal goods no longer served a useful purpose or were broken, they were readily discarded by the Caddo, perhaps because they could be easily replaced.

One site from the pueblo of Nacogdoches (see Figure 5.3), reoccupied in 1779 by Gil Ybarbo and settlers at the site of the former Mission Nuestra Señora de los Nacogdoches (abandoned in 1772), contains both Caddo and European ceramics and other European goods (most notably glass beads and the bones of domestic animals). The contexts suggest considerable interaction throughout much of the

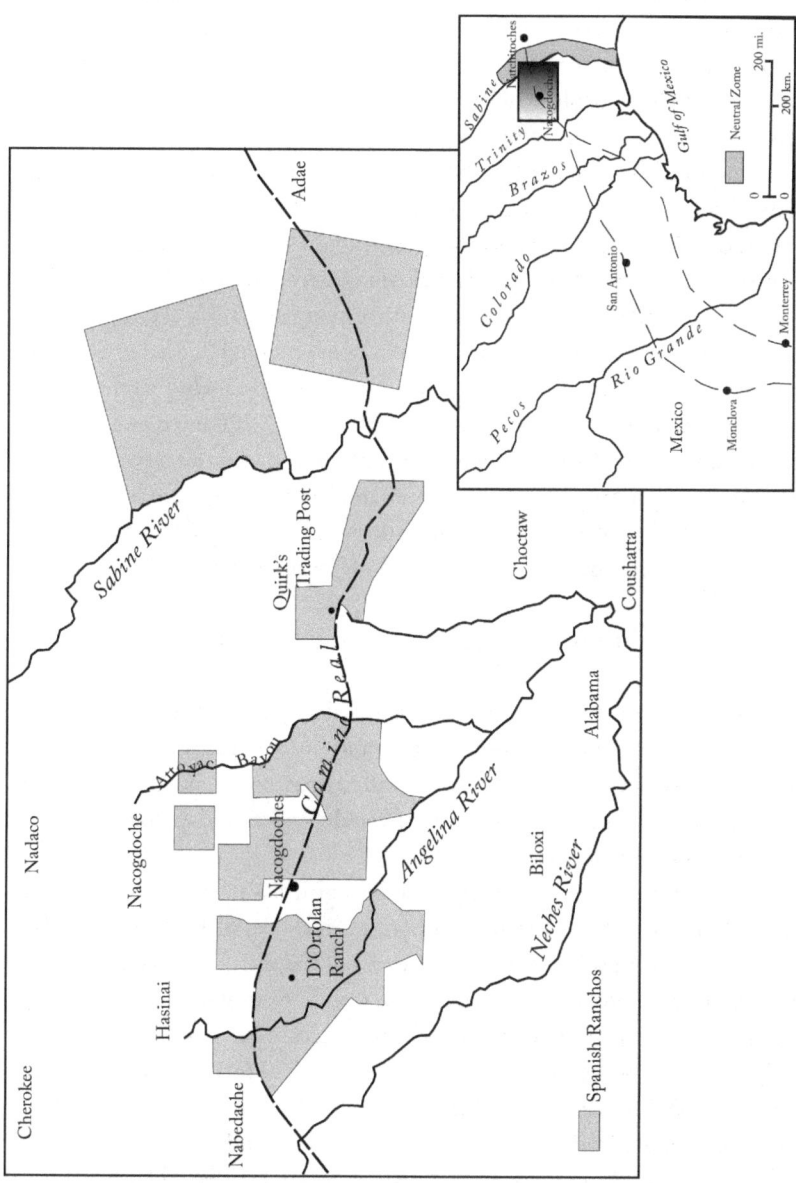

5.3. Late-18th- and early-19th-century Spanish ranchos and the locations of aboriginal groups around the Pueblo of Nacogdoches in east Texas

market economy period between Caddo groups living around Nacogdoches and the Spanish and Mexican settlers and ranchers (Ewers 1969). This is not surprising since Nacogdoches was at that time a local center of European commerce and trade. European ceramics found at this site included creamware and pearlware vessel sherds in abundance, as well as faience brune and Mexican majolica, and sherds from reconstructable Caddo vessels (Tom Middlebrook 2007, personal communication); these vessels probably held items such as bear fat and corn traded and bartered with the citizens of Nacogdoches.

The Bernardo D'Ortolan ranch (1796–1813) was an outpost west of the pueblo (see Figure 5.3), and one of the many large ranchos established by the Spanish government around Nacogdoches. The floor of the main structure at the ranch contained plain and brushed Caddo ceramics along with European-made artifacts typical of those found elsewhere in colonial New Spain and Texas (Perttula 2008). D'Ortolan, like other Europeans living in this frontier economy (Girard et al. 2008), was probably heavily involved in the trade with local Indians, including the Caddo. In 1828, skins from more than 40,000 deer, 1,500 bear, 1,200 otter, and 600 beaver were traded by Indians in Nacogdoches, although the trade in livestock was probably a more important part of the frontier market economy at that time. Even General Terán, the Mexican envoy on an inspection tour, considered the trade to be important to the commerce of the Province of Texas (Ewers 1969:47 n. 27).

Cultural Identity, Leaders, and Location

The Caddo existed for hundreds of years as politically autonomous groups and also thrived as successful agriculturalists, maintaining a viable social order based on hierarchical, organizational, and administrative structures. Underlying contemporary Caddo identity is the historical role of Caddo leaders and diplomats and the groups' connection to place (Carter 1995).

Consensus building and the management of political and economic structures was the work of the *caddi,* a position authorized in stories of Caddo origins (see Dorsey 1905:7–13). In spite of the disjunctive and fragmenting effects of disease on the stability of different Caddo groups, the Caddo were able to maintain a coherent cultural identity through the underlying structure and continuity of strong leadership (Carter 1995; Smith 1991, 1995). From 1770 to 1800 the Kadohadacho had only two *caddices* (political leaders) that led the people, and Dehahuit, another strong Caddo leader, took over soon after that and led the people until his death in 1833. Caddo groups were disproportionately affected by European-introduced diseases and these diseases, according to General Terán, "have wreaked great havoc in the tribe" (Jackson 2000:80). Dehahuit, who was lucky to have survived a case of smallpox (Jackson 2000:80), filled the leadership vacuum left by the absence of Hasinai leaders and represented these groups in negotiations with the Texas governor in 1809 (Smith 1991:196–198).

The *caddi* were also positioned as religious leaders in Caddo society. After Mexico won its independence in 1821, it immediately sent a notice asking the tribes of Texas to "unite with the empire, promising them equal rights and privileges as citizens, a liberal system of government, and protection" (Carter 1995:257). Dehahuit's reply offered support, but only under certain conditions. These included that the Caddo not be required to accept the Catholic religion. Missionaries had sought to transform traditional Caddo practices, from the "savage" into a "civilized" Spanish citizen. Dehahuit negotiated allegiances and alliances, but ultimately rejected the accompanying social policy sought by the Spanish and Mexican governments, preferring to maintain the bedrock-strong Caddo cultural identity.

Cultural identity may be defined as a collective true self, one that people with a shared ancestry and Indian history hold in common. As the title of Cecile Elkins Carter's (1995) book *Where We Come From* suggests, Caddo cultural identity was inherently tied to place. Although the French and the Spanish claimed to possess Caddo country, neither denied Caddo land rights. In practice, this changed considerably with the arrival of Americans and Texans. In 1828, the Grand Caddo, asserting this claim to lands in east Texas, stated, in a reply to a question posed by General Manuel de Mier y Terán about land rights, that "he [Grand Caddo] was not in Mexican territory nor that of the North Americans, but in his own land, which was nothing else but his" (Carter 1995:261; Jackson 2000:80). The Caddo American colonial experience was a struggle to maintain rights to their traditional lands.

Conclusion

Sustained contact between the Caddo peoples and the Spanish, French, Mexican, Texan, and U.S. governments brought European trade materials and technology in tandem with the social objectives and policies of these foreign polities, many aimed at replacing Caddo cultural identity under the guise of religious conversion, trade, and participation as consumers in a burgeoning market economy, albeit one of relatively small scale at the time. Ultimately, the aim of dispossession of Caddo lands was achieved by Texans and Americans, who sought these rich lands in what became Arkansas, Louisiana, Oklahoma, and Texas. However, the strong leadership of various *caddices* was based on long-standing commonalities and alliances between kin-related Caddo groups and families and an appreciation for trade and exchange that was, prior to European contact, solidly based on kin and gender relationships and reciprocity. Under this leadership, Caddo groups and families coalesced as the primary means of maintaining their cultural identity and assuring their survival in a chaotic world. The population of Caddo groups continued to decrease because of prolonged exposure to European epidemic diseases, from roughly 28,000 in the late 17th century to about 500 people when they left the Brazos reserve in the summer of 1859 (see Table 5.2). However, they continued to be important participants in the Texas and Louisiana market economies through the 1830s. For example, upon a request from the United States to allow other tribes to enter their lands, in effect asking that they share their limited resources, the Caddo demanded compensation. Dehahuit stipulated that an annuity be paid in return for allowing other tribes to reside alongside the Caddo (Carter 1995:259). Cultural identity was built on the strength of Caddo relationships to their land, and they insisted upon fair treatment in the frontier market economy, as long as they were able to hold on to those lands. Everything changed for the Caddo peoples after 1835.

To date, archaeology is a poor attendant to this period of Caddo strife and turmoil. It may be that Kadohadacho sites such as Timber Hill are not the prototype for this period; we simply do not know. It may also be the case that archaeologists have been uninterested in searching for sites of this period, focusing instead on the many prehistoric Caddo sites with impressive mounds and burial grounds. Regardless, from 1835 to the present the U.S. government has done little to acknowledge the Caddo presence in east Texas and surrounding areas. For the most part, disregard has followed displacement. As archaeologists, it is surely important to make sure we are not complicit in this denying of Caddo cultural identity and their abiding connection to traditional homelands. Working to locate archaeological sites that date to this period is one course of action archaeologists can take toward reaffirming that the Caddo as a living people have an identity in east Texas.

The study of late-18th- through mid-19th-century Caddo archaeology does not currently contribute as much as it could to a broader understanding of culture contact during the era of the frontier market, despite a fairly rich archival record, at least in some respects. As stated above, the archaeology for this period is nearly invisible. This sad state of archaeological affairs was lamented more than 15 years ago (Perttula 1992:239–240), but little has changed. Archaeologists have played a haphazard role in Texas with respect to the acknowledgment and regard for the Caddo presence here and their connections to the history of Texas, as illustrated by the current state of archaeological knowledge about the Caddo in historic times.

Archaeologists in Texas continue to play a role in a postcolonial enterprise, that enterprise being Texas, a world unto its own. We think about the words of Don Birchfield (1998:139–140), an Oklahoma Choctaw anthropologist, who recently pointed out in his book *The Oklahoma Basic Intelligence Test* that Texans "seem to be incapable of thinking of Indians as Texans . . . To Texans, Indians have always been a part of nature; they are sub-human. They are also past tense . . . They were dealt with long ago . . . they are gone now; no need to dwell on why or how that happened, unless, of course, Hollywood might be interested."

The Caddo did not stand a chance of living in peace in Texas when the United States and Texas began land expropriations of the rich farmlands and woodlands that were where the Caddo's homes stood. This was disastrous for the Caddo, and led to their eventual harried and forced removal from their homelands. Within a generation of settling boundary disputes with the United States in 1835, and after attempting to cling to lands within the new Republic of Texas, the Caddo were gone from all of Texas. It is our hope that Caddo archaeologists will work to renew support for Indian history and descendant groups and their enduring connection to the traditional homelands of the Caddo.

Acknowledgments

We appreciate the opportunity provided by Lance Greene and Mark R. Plane to participate in their symposium at the 2007 Society for American Archaeology meetings and to contribute this paper. Thanks to Tom Middlebrook for information about recent archaeological findings in Nacogdoches, Texas. Sandra Hannum prepared Figure 5.2.

References

Adair, James
  1930 Adair's History of the American Indians. Samuel Cole Williams, ed. Johnson
  [1775] City, TN: Watauga Press.
Adams, William, and Sarah Boling
  1989 Status and Ceramics for Planters and Slaves on Three Georgia Coastal Plantations. Historical Archaeology 23(1):69–96.
Adelman, Jeremy, and Stephen Aron
  1999 From Borderlands to Borders: Empires, Nation-States, and the Peoples in Between in North American History. American Historical Review 104:815–816.
American State Papers, Indian Affairs
  1832 American State Papers, Indian Affairs [1789–1827]. 2 vols. Washington, DC:
  –34 Gales and Seaton.
Anderson, Benedict
  1991 Imagined Communities: Reflections on the Origin and Spread of Nationalism. London: Verso.
Anderson, Gary
  2005 The Conquest of Texas: Ethnic Cleansing in the Promised Land, 1820–1875. Norman: University of Oklahoma Press.
Appadurai, Arjun
  1986 Introduction: Commodities and the Politics of Value. *In* The Social Life of Things: Commodities in Cultural Perspective. Arjun Appadurai, ed. Pp. 3–63. Cambridge: Cambridge University Press.
Ascher, Robert, and Charles Fairbanks
  1971 Excavation of a Slave Cabin: Georgia, U.S.A. Historical Archaeology 5(1):3–17.
Au, Dennis
  1995 François Deloeuil Site (20MR229): Field Notes on the Features. Manuscript in possession of the author.
Baird, James M.
  2006 Paternalism and Profits: Planters and Overseers in Piedmont Virginia, 1750–1825. *In* Cultures and Identities in Colonial British America. Robert Olwell and Alan Tully, eds. Pp.147–168. Baltimore: Johns Hopkins University Press.
Baker, Steven
  1972 Colono-Indian Pottery from Cambridge, South Carolina with Comments on the Historic Catawba Pottery Trade. Institute of Archeology and Anthropology, University of South Carolina Notebook 4(1):3–30.
  1976 The Historic Catawba Peoples: Exploratory Perspectives in Ethnohistory and Ar-

chaeology. Report prepared for Duke Power Co. Manuscript on file, Department of History, University of South Carolina, Columbia.

Bamforth, Douglas B.
1988 Ecology and Human Organization on the Great Plains. New York: Plenum Press.

Banks, Marcus
1996 Ethnicity: Anthropological Constructions. London: Routledge.

Barnard, Andrew
1840 Letter to Governor Edward Dudley, April 6, 1840. Governor's papers, State Archives, Raleigh, North Carolina.

Barnes, Bettina
1975 Irish Traveling People. In Gypsies, Tinkers, and Other Travelers. Farnhm Rehfisch, ed. Pp. 231–256. London: Academic Press.

Barnhart, John, and Dorothy Riker
1971 Indiana to 1816: The Colonial Period. Indiana Historical Bureau and Indiana Historical Society, Indianapolis.

Barr, Juliana
2004 A Diplomacy of Gender: Rituals of First Contact in the "Land of the Tejas." William and Mary Quarterly 61:393–437.
2005 Beyond Their Control: Spaniards in Native Texas. In Choice, Persuasion, and Coercion: Social Control on Spain's North American Frontiers. J. F. de la Teja and R. Frank, eds. Pp. 149–177. Albuquerque: University of New Mexico Press.
2007 Peace Came in the Form of a Woman: Indians and Spaniards in the Texas Borderlands. Chapel Hill: University of North Carolina Press.

Barth, Fredrik
1969 Introduction. In Ethnic Groups and Boundaries: The Social Organization of Culture Difference. F. Barth, ed. Pp. 9–38. Oslo: Scandinavian University Books.

Barthes, Roland
1993 Mythologies. Annette Lavers, trans. London: Vintage Books.

Beaudry, Mary, and Stephen Mrozowski
1988 Interdisciplinary Investigations of the Boott Mills, Lowell, Massachusetts, vol. 1: Life at the Boarding Houses, A Preliminary Report. National Park Service, Boston.
2001 Cultural Space and Worker Identity in the Company City: Nineteenth-Century Lowell, Massachusetts. Cambridge: Cambridge University Press.

Benson, Maxine
1988 From Pittsburgh to the Rocky Mountains: Major Stephen Long's Expedition 1819–1820. Golden, CO: Fulcrum.

Bentley, G. Carter
1987 Ethnicity and Practice. Comparative Studies in Society and History 33:169–175.

Bentley, M. M.
1991 The Slaveholding Catawbas. South Carolina Historical Magazine 92:85–98.

Bergmann, William H.
2005 Commerce and Arms: The Federal Government, Native Americans, and the Economy of the Old Northwest, 1783–1807. Ph.D. dissertation, University of Cincinnati. Ann Arbor: University Microfilms.

References

Berkhofer, Robert F.
  1978 The White Man's Indian: Images of the American Indian from Columbus to the Present. New York: Random House.
Berkson, Alice
  1992 Cultural Resistance of the Prairie Kickapoo at the Grand Village, McLean County, Illinois. Illinois Archaeology 4(2):109–205.
Bhabha, Homi K.
  1994 The Location of Culture. London: Routledge.
Bieder, Robert E.
  1986 Science Encounters the Indian, 1820–1880: The Early Years of American Ethnology. Norman: University of Oklahoma Press.
Biggs, William
  1977 Narrative of William Biggs, while he was a Prisoner with the Kickepoo Indians.
  [1825] The Garland Library of Narratives of North American Indian Captivities, vol. 37. New York: Garland Publishing.
Binford, Lewis R.
  1983 In Pursuit of the Past: Decoding the Archaeological Record. Berkeley: University of California Press.
Binnema, Theodore
  2001 Common and Contested Ground: A Human and Environmental History of the Northwestern Plains. Norman: University of Oklahoma Press.
Birchfield, D. L.
  1998 The Oklahoma Basic Intelligence Test. Greenfield, NY: Greenfield Review Press.
Blakeslee, Donald J.
  1995 Along Ancient Trails: The Mallet Expedition of 1739. Niwot: University Press of Colorado.
Blumer, Thomas J.
  2004 Catawba Indian Pottery. Tuscaloosa: The University of Alabama Press.
Bollwerk, Elizabeth
  2007 Negotiating with Nicotiana: An Investigation of the Role of Tobacco Smoking and Pipes in Native and European Relations in the Middle Atlantic. Paper presented at the 72nd Annual Meeting of the Society for American Archaeology, Austin, Texas.
Bolton, H. E., ed.
  1914 Athanase de Mezieres and the Louisiana-Texas Frontier, 1768–1780. 2 vols. Cleveland: Clark Publishing.
Bond, Beverly
  1923 Two Westward Journeys of John Filson, 1785. Mississippi Valley Historical Review 9(4):320–330.
Bourdieu, Pierre
  1977 Outline of a Theory of Practice. Cambridge: Cambridge University Press.
Boutton, Thomas W., M. J. Lynott, and M. P. Bumsted
  1991 Stable Carbon Isotopes and the Study of Prehistoric Human Diet. Critical Reviews in Food Science and Nutrition 30:373–385.

Boydston, Jeanne
   1990   Home and Work: Housework, Wages, and the Ideology of Labor in the Early Republic. New York: Oxford University Press.

Bozell, John. R., J. Ludwickson, and L. L. Tieszen
   1997   Appendix D: Stable Isotope Measurements on Archeological Bison in Nebraska. *In* Bioarchaeology of the North Central United States. D. W. Owsley and J. C. Rose, eds. Pp. 337. Arkansas Archeological Survey Research Series No. 49.

Brain, Jeffrey P.
   1979   Tunica Treasure. Papers of the Peabody Museum of Archaeology and Ethnology, vol. 71. Cambridge, Massachusetts.

Branstner, Mark, and Terrance Martin
   1987   Working Class Detroit: Late Victorian Consumer Choices and Status. *In* Consumer Choice in Historical Archaeology. Suzanne Spencer-Wood, ed. Pp. 301–320. New York: Plenum Press.

Browder, Nathaniel
   1973   The Cherokees and Those Who Came After. Hayesville, NC.

Brown, Douglas S.
   1966   The Catawba Indians: The People of the River. Chapel Hill: University of North Carolina Press.

Bruck, Joanna
   2007   Ritual and Rationality. *In* The Archaeology of Identities: A Reader. Timothy Insoll, ed. Pp. 281–307. London: Routledge.

Bullock, Steven C.
   1996   Revolutionary Brotherhood: Freemasonry and the Transformation of the American Social Order, 1730–1840. Chapel Hill: University of North Carolina Press.

Burley, David V.
   1988   Function, Meaning, and Context: Ambiguities in Ceramic Use by the Hivernant Métis of the Northwestern Plains. Historical Archaeology 23:97–106.

Burley, David V., Gayel A. Horsfall, and John D. Brandon
   1992   Structural Considerations of Métis Ethnicity: An Archaeological, Architectural, and Historical Study. Vermillion: University of South Dakota Press.

Burris, Lucy
   2006   People of the Poudre: An Ethnohistory of the Cache la Poudre River National Heritage Area, A.D. 1500–1880. National Park Service, United States Department of the Interior, and Friends of the Poudre and Cache la Poudre River National Heritage Area.

Bush, Leslie
   2007   Appendix B: Floral Remains. *In* Report of the 2006 Archaeological Investigations at Kethtippecanunk (12-T-59), Tippecanoe County, Indiana, by Michael Strezewski, Robert G. McCullough, Dorothea McCullough, Craig Arnold, and Josh Wells. Indiana University-Purdue University Fort Wayne Archaeological Survey, Reports of Investigations 703. Report submitted to the Indiana Department of Natural Resources, Division of Historic Preservation and Archaeology, Indianapolis.

Byerly, Ryan M., and David J. Meltzer
  2005 Historic Period Faunal Remains from Mustang Springs on the Southern Plains of Texas. Plains Anthropologist 50(194):1–18.
Bynum, John Gray
  1838 Letter to General Winfield Scott, June 13, 1838. William Preston Bynum Papers, Southern Historical Collection. Chapel Hill: University of North Carolina.
Byrd, William
  1967 History of the Dividing Line Betwixt North Carolina and Virginia. New York: Courier Dover Publications.
Caddo Chiefs
  1837 Petition, Caddo Chiefs to Joel Poinsett, January 9, 1837, in Letters Received by the Office of Indian Affairs, 1824–1881. Roll 31, Caddo Agency, 1824–1842.
Calhoun, Craig
  1994 Nationalism. Minneapolis: University of Minnesota Press.
Calloway, C. G.
  2003 One Vast Winter Count: The Native American West before Lewis and Clark. Lincoln: University of Nebraska Press.
Carlson, S.
  1996 Where in the World (System) Are the Texas Missions? Southern Studies: An Interdisciplinary Journal of the South 7(1):1–24.
Carter, C. E.
  1995 Caddo Indians: Where We Come From. Norman: University of Oklahoma Press.
Carter, Harvey L.
  1965 William H. Ashley. In Mountain Men & Fur Trappers of the Far West. LeRoy R. Hafen, ed. Pp. 79–90. Lincoln: University of Nebraska Press.
Cherokee County Register of Deeds
  1839 Cherokee County, North Carolina deed records, Book 1, pp. 205–212.
Chipman, Donald E.
  1992 Spanish Texas, 1519–1821. Austin: University of Texas Press.
Chisholm, B., J. Driver, S. Dube, and H. Swartz
  1986 Assessment of Prehistoric Bison Foraging and Movement Patterns via Stable-Carbon Isotope Analysis. Plains Anthropologist 31:193–206.
Clark, Christopher
  1996 The Consequences of the Market Revolution in the American North. In The Market Revolution in America: Social, Political, and Religious Expressions, 1800–1880. Melvyn Stokes and Stephen Conway, eds. Pp. 23–42. Charlottesville: University Press of Virginia.
Clark, William
  1949 Journal of William Clark from the 1791 Scott/Wilkinson Expedition to the Wabash. Draper manuscripts, Roll 63J:138–150.
Coke, Thomas
  1791 Journal entry, quoted in Douglas S. Brown, The Catawba Indians: The People of the River. Pp. 288. Chapel Hill: University of North Carolina Press, 1966.

Conn, Steven
    2004   History's Shadow: Native Americans and Historical Consciousness in the Nineteenth Century. Chicago: University of Chicago Press.

Cooke, Sarah E., and Rachel B. Ramadhyani
    1993   Indians and a Changing Frontier: The Art of George Winter. Indianapolis: Indiana Historical Society.

Cott, Nancy
    1977   The Bonds of Womanhood: "Woman's Sphere" in New England, 1780–1835. New Haven: Yale University Press.

Cotter, John
    1958   Archaeological Investigations at Jamestown Colonial National Historical Park and Jamestown National Historic Site, Virginia. National Park Service, Archaeological Research Series 4. Washington, DC.

Cumming, William P.
    1958   The Discoveries of John Lederer. Charlottesville: University Press of Virginia.

Cunningham, Wilbur M., ed.
    1967   The Letter Book of William Burnett: Early Fur Trader in the Land of the Four Flags. Fort Miami Heritage Society of Michigan.

Currey, Benjamin
    1835   Letter to Lewis Cass, September 7, 1835. *In* Letters Received by the Office of Indian Affairs 1824–1881, Microcopy 234, Record Group 75, United States National Archives and Records Administration, Washington, DC.

Davis, R. P. Stephen Jr., and Brett H. Riggs
    2004   An Introduction to the Catawba Project. North Carolina Archaeology 53:1–41.

De Cunzo, Lu Ann
    1987   Adapting to Factory and City: Illustrations from the Industrialization and Urbanization of Paterson, New Jersey. *In* Consumer Choice in Historical Archaeology. Suzanne Spencer-Wood, ed. Pp. 261–296. New York: Plenum Press.

Deetz, James
    1996   In Small Things Forgotten: An Archaeology of Early American Life, revised and expanded edition. New York: Anchor Books.

Deloria, Philip J.
    1998   Playing Indian. New Haven: Yale University Press.

Derrick, S. M., and D. E. Wilson
    2001   The Effects of Epidemic Disease on Caddo Demographic Structure. Bulletin of the Texas Archeological Society 72:91–103.

Detroit Indian Department
    1790   Document Indicating Presents Distributed from Detroit and its Dependencies, July 15, 1790. Microcopy 588, Roll 7, Record Group 59, United States National Archives and Records Administration, Washington, DC.

Dickens, Roy
    1979   The Origins and Development of Cherokee Culture. *In* The Cherokee Indian Nation: A Troubled History. Duane King, ed. Pp. 3–32. Knoxville: University of Tennessee Press.

Dietler, Michael
   2007   Culinary Encounters: Food, Identity, and Colonialism. *In* The Archaeology of Food and Identity. Katheryn C. Twiss, ed. Pp. 218–242. Center for Archaeological Investigations Occasional Paper No. 34. Carbondale: Southern Illinois University.

Dobbs, Clark A.
   1975   12-T-59: A Preliminary Report on the Van Natta Site. Manuscript on file, Glenn A. Black Laboratory of Archaeology, Indiana University, Bloomington.

Dorsey, George A.
   1905   Traditions of the Caddo. Publication No. 41. Carnegie Institution of Washington, Washington, DC.

Douglas, Mary, and Baron Isherwood
   1996   The World of Goods: Towards an Anthropology of Consumption. London: Routledge.

Draper Manuscripts
   1949   Draper Manuscript Collection [microform]. Department of Photographic Reproduction, University of Chicago.

Driver, Harold E.
   1961   Indians of North America. Chicago: University of Chicago Press.

Drooker, Penelope B.
   2004   Pipes, Leadership, and Interregional Interaction in Protohistoric Midwestern and Northeastern North America. *In* Smoking and Culture: The Archaeology of Tobacco Pipes in Eastern North America. Sean Rafferty and Rob Mann, eds. Pp. 73–124. Knoxville: University of Tennessee Press.

Du Dauphine, Durand
   1934   A Huguenot Exile in Virginia; Or, Voyages of a Frenchman Exiled for His Re-
   [1687] gion, with a Description of Virginia and Maryland. G. Chinard, ed. and trans. New York: Press of the Pioneer.

Eddy, Frank
   1982   The Archaeological Mitigation Program and Excavations at Site 5MF605, Browns Park National Wildlife Refuge, Moffat County, Colorado. Prepared for United States Department of the Interior National Park Service, Rocky Mountain Regional Office Interagency Archaeological Services Branch.

Egloff, Keith T.
   1992   The Late Woodland Period in Southwestern Virginia. *In* Middle and Late Woodland Research in Virginia: A Synthesis. Thomas R. Reinhert and Mary N. Hodges, eds. Pp. 187–233. Special Publication 29. Archaeological Society of Virginia, Richmond.

Ehrhardt, Kathleen L.
   2005   European Metals in Native Hands: Rethinking the Dynamics of Technological Change, 1640–1683. Tuscaloosa: The University of Alabama Press.

Epperson, Terrence
   1999   The Contested Commons: Archaeologies of Race, Repression, and Resistance

in New York City. *In* Historical Archaeologies of Capitalism. Mark Leone and Parker Potter Jr., eds. Pp. 81–110. New York: Kluwer Academic/Plenum Publishers.

Ethridge, Robbie
- 2006 Creating the Shatter Zone: Indian Slave Traders and the Collapse of the Southeastern Chiefdoms. *In* Light on the Path: The Anthropology and History of the Southeastern Indians. Thomas J. Pluckhahn and Robbie Ethridge, eds. Pp. 207–218. Tuscaloosa: The University of Alabama Press.

Ewers, John C., ed.
- 1969 The Indians of Texas in 1830 by Jean Louis Berlandier. Washington, DC: Smithsonian Institution Press.

Faith, J. Tyler, and Adam D. Gordon
- 2007 Skeletal Element Abundances in Archaeofaunal Assemblages: Economic Utility, Sample Size, and Assessment of Carcass Transport Strategies. Journal of Archaeological Science 34:872–882.

Fanon, Frantz
- 1968 The Wretched of the Earth. New York: Grove Press.

Ferguson, Brian R., and Neil L. Whitehead, eds.
- 1999 The Violent Edge of Empire. *In* War in the Tribal Zone: Expanding States and Indigenous Warfare, 2nd edition. Pp. 1–30. Santa Fe: School of American Research.

Ferguson, Leland
- 1989 Lowcountry Plantations, the Catawba Nation, and River Burnished Pottery. *In* Studies in South Carolina Archaeology: Essays in Honor of Robert L. Stephenson. Albert C. Goodyear III and Glen T. Hanson, eds. Pp. 185–192. South Carolina Institute of Archaeology and Anthropology Research Papers 10. Occasional Papers of the South Carolina Institute of Archaeology and Anthropology, University of South Carolina, Columbia.
- 1992 Uncommon Ground: Archaeology and Early African America, 1650–1800. Washington, DC: Smithsonian Institution Press.

Fewkes, Vladimir
- 1944 Catawba Pottery-Making, with Notes on Pamunkey Pottery-Making, Cherokee Pottery-Making and Coiling. Proceedings of the American Philosophical Society 88(2):69–124.

Finger, John R.
- 1984 The Eastern Band of Cherokee Indians 1819–1900. Knoxville: University of Tennessee Press.

Fitts, Mary E.
- 2006 Mapping Catawba Coalescence. North Carolina Archaeology 55:1–59.

Flores, Dan L.
- 2005 Jefferson's Grand Expedition and the Mystery of the Red River. *In* A Whole Country in Commotion: The Louisiana Purchase and the American Southwest. Patrick G. Williams, S. Charles Bolton, and Jeannie M. Whayne, eds. Pp. 21–40. Fayetteville: University of Arkansas Press.

Flores, Dan L., ed.
- 1984 Jefferson & Southwestern Exploration: The Freeman & Custis Accounts of the Red River Expedition of 1806. Norman: University of Oklahoma Press.
- 1985 Journal of an Indian Trader: Anthony Glass and the Texas Trading Frontier, 1790–1810. College Station: Texas A&M University Press.

Flower, George
- 1882 History of the English Settlement in Edwards County, Illinois, Founded in 1817 and 1818 by Morris Birkbeck and George Flower. Chicago Historical Society's Collection, vol. 1. Chicago: Fergus Printing.

Foucault, Michel
- 1972 The Archaeology of Knowledge. A. M. Sheridan Smith, trans. New York: Pantheon Books.
- 1978 The History of Sexuality, vol. 1: An Introduction. Robert Hurley, trans. New York: Random House.
- 1979 Discipline and Punish: The Birth of the Prison. Alan Sheridan, trans. New York: Vintage Books.

Frederic, Daniel
- 1882 Colonial Days and Tobacco. Popular Monthly 14(4):531–546.

Freeman-Witthoft, Bonita
- 1988 Formal Games in the Cherokee Ritual Cycle. Expedition 30(2):53–60.

Frémont, John C.
- 1845 Map of an Exploring Expedition to the Rocky Mountains in the Year 1842, and to Oregon and North California in the Years 1843–44. Baltimore: Lithograph by E. Weber and Company.

Gallivan, Martin
- 2003 James River Chiefdoms. Lincoln: University of Nebraska Press.

Galloway, Patricia
- 2006 Practicing Ethnohistory: Mining Archives, Hearing Testimony, Constructing Narrative. Lincoln: University of Nebraska Press.

Garrow, Patrick H., and Thomas R. Wheaton
- 1989 Colonoware Ceramics: The Evidence from Yaughan and Curriboo Plantations. *In* Studies in South Carolina Archaeology: Essays in Honor of Robert L. Stephenson. Albert C. Goodyear III and Glen T. Hanson, eds. Pp. 175–184. South Carolina Institute of Archaeology and Anthropology Research Papers 10. Occasional Papers of the South Carolina Institute of Archaeology and Anthropology, University of South Carolina, Columbia.

Gauthier-Larouche, Georges
- 1974 Évolution de la Maison Rurale Traditionnelle dans le Région de Québec. Québec: Les Presses De L'Université Laval.

Genovese, Eugene
- 1965 The Political Economy of Slavery; Studies in the Economy and Society of the Slave South. New York: Vintage Books.

Girard, J. S., R. C. Vogel, and H. E. Jackson
- 2008 History and Archaeology of the Pierre Robleau Household and Bayou Pierre

Community: Perspectives on Rural Society and Economy in Northwest Louisiana at the Time of the Freeman & Custis Expedition. *In* Freeman and Custis Red River Expedition of 1806: Two Hundred Years Later. F. C. Hardy, ed. Pp. 147–180. Bulletin of the Museum of Life Sciences, No. 14. Museum of Life Sciences, Louisiana State University, Shreveport.

Godbold, E. Stanly, Jr., and Mattie Russell
 1990 Confederate Colonel and Cherokee Chief: The Life of William Holland Thomas. Knoxville: University of Tennessee Press.

Goodman, Jordan
 1994 Tobacco in History: Cultures of Dependence. London: Routledge.

Goodwin, Gerald
 1973 Christianity, Civilization, and the Savage: The Anglican Mission to the American Indian. Historical Magazine of the Protestant Episcopal Church 42(2):93–110.

Goodwin, Lorinda B. R.
 1999 An Archaeology of Manners: The Polite World of the Merchant Elite of Colonial Massachusetts. New York: Kluwer Academic/Plenum Publishers.

Gosden, Chris
 2001 Postcolonial Archaeology: Issues of Culture, Identity, and Knowledge. *In* Archaeological Theory Today. Ian Hodder, ed. Pp. 241–262. Malden, MA: Blackwell Publishers.
 2004 Archaeology and Colonialism: Cultural Contact from 5000 B.C. to the Present. Cambridge: Cambridge University Press.

Grand Lodge of Free and Accepted Masons of the State of Michigan
 2007 Some Background for an Aspirant. Electronic document, http://www.gl-mi.org/, accessed May 1, 2007.

Greene, Lance
 2005 Race, Class, and Material Culture in Antebellum North Carolina. Paper presented at the Southeastern Archaeological Conference, Columbia, South Carolina.

Gregory, Anne K.
 1925 Notes on Sewee Indians and Indian Remains of Christ Church Parish, Charleston County, South Carolina. Contributions from the Charleston Museum 5. Charleston, South Carolina.

Gregory, H. F., George Avery, Aubra L. Lee, and Jay C. Blaine
 2004 Presidio Los Adaes: Spanish, French, and Caddoan Interaction on the Northern Frontier. Historical Archaeology 38(3):65–77.

Grumet, Robert S.
 1995 Historic Contact: Indian People and Colonists in Today's Northeastern United States in the Sixteenth through Eighteenth Centuries. Norman: University of Oklahoma Press.

Guilds, John Caldwell
 2003 A Literary View. *In* An Early and Strong Sympathy: The Indian Writings of William Gilmore Simms. John Caldwell Guilds and Charles Hudson, eds. Pp. xiii–xxxiii. Columbia: University of South Carolina Press.

Haefeli, Evan
  1999   A Note on the Use of North American Borderlands. American Historical Review 104:1222–1225.
Haggard, J. V.
  1942   The Neutral Ground between Louisiana and Texas, 1806–1821. Ph.D. dissertation, Department of History, University of Texas, Austin.
  1945   The House of Barr and Davenport. Southwestern Historical Quarterly 49(1):66–88.
Hall, Jonathon M.
  1997   Ethnic Identity in Greek Antiquity. Cambridge: Cambridge University Press.
Hämäläinen, Pekka
  1998   The Western Comanche Trade Center: Rethinking the Plains Indian Trade System. Western Historical Quarterly 29(4):485–513.
Hamilton, T. M., and K. O. Emery
  1988   Eighteenth-Century Gunflints from Fort Michilimackinac and Other Colonial Sites. Archaeological Completion Report Series No. 13, Mackinac Island State Park Commission, Mackinac Island, Michigan.
Harrington, Jean C.
  1952   Glassmaking at Jamestown: America's First Industry. Richmond, VA: Dietz Press.
Harrington, Jean C., Albert Manucy, and John Goggin
  1956   Archaeological Excavations in the Courtyard of Castillo de San Marcos, St. Augustine, Florida. St. Augustine Historical Society.
Harrington, Mark R.
  1908   Catawba Potters and Their Work. American Anthropologist 10(3):399–407.
Hatfield, April Lee
  2004   Atlantic Virginia: Intercolonial Relations in the Seventeenth Century. Philadelphia: University of Pennsylvania Press.
Heath, Charles L.
  2004   Catawba Militarism: An Ethnohistorical and Archaeological Overview. North Carolina Archaeology 53:80–121.
Hegmon, Michelle
  1998   Technology, Style, and Social Practices: Archaeological Approaches. In The Archaeology of Social Boundaries. Miriam T. Stark, ed. Pp. 264–280. Washington, DC: Smithsonian Institution Press.
Hill, Sarah
  1997   Weaving New Worlds: Southeastern Cherokee Women and Their Basketry. Chapel Hill: University of North Carolina Press.
Hindman, Thomas C.
  1841   Letter to Commissioner of Indian Affairs T. Hartley Crawford. December 20, Letters Received by the Office of Indian Affairs (1824–1881), Microfilm 234(86):584–587, Record Group 75, United States National Archives and Records Administration, Washington, DC.
Hudson, Charles M.
  1970   The Catawba Nation. Athens: University of Georgia Press.

1990 The Juan Pardo Expeditions: Exploration of the Carolinas and Tennessee, 1566–1568. Washington, DC: Smithsonian Institution Press.

1997 Knights of Spain, Warriors of the Sun. Athens: University of Georgia Press.

2003 An Ethnohistorical View. *In* An Early and Strong Sympathy: The Indian Writings of William Gilmore Simms. John Caldwell Guilds and Charles Hudson, eds. Pp. xxxiv–li. Columbia: University of South Carolina Press.

Huebner, J. A., and T. W. Boutton

1994 The Isotopic Ecology and Niche Separation of Grassland Herbivores in a Prehistoric Central Texas Ecotone. *In* Human Ecology in the Middle Onion Creek Valley. R. Ricklis and M. Collins, eds. Pp. 569–582. Studies in Archeology 19, Texas Archeological Research Laboratory, Austin, Texas.

Hutchison, David

1843 Letter, quoted in Douglas S. Brown, The Catawba Indians: The People of the River. Pp. 291–292. Chapel Hill: University of North Carolina Press, 1966.

Imlay, George

1916 A Topographical Description of the Western Territory of North America, 1793. *In* Indiana as Seen by Early Travelers: A Collection of Reprints from Books of Travel, Letters, and Diaries Prior to 1830. Harlow Lindley, ed. Pp. 9–16. Indianapolis: Indiana Historical Commission.

Inscoe, John

1996 Mountain Masters: Slavery and the Sectional Crisis in Western North Carolina. Knoxville: University of Tennessee Press.

Jablow, Joseph

1950 The Cheyenne in Plains Indian Trade Relations 1795–1840. Lincoln: University of Nebraska Press.

Jackson, J.

2005 Indian Agent: Peter Ellis Bean in Mexican Texas. College Station: Texas A&M University Press.

Jackson, J., ed.

2000 Texas by Terán: The Diary Kept by General Manuel de Mier y Terán on His 1828 Inspection of Texas. Austin: University of Texas Press.

2003 Almonte's Texas: Juan N. Almonte's 1834 Inspection, Secret Report & Role in the 1836 Campaign. Texas State Historical Association, Austin.

Jacobs, W. R., ed.

1967 The Appalachian Indian Frontier: The Edmond Atkin Report and Plan of 1755. Lincoln: University of Nebraska Press.

Jelks, E. B.

2002 The Caddo. Journal of Northeast Texas Archaeology 16:1–28.

Jones, Brian, Jason Mancini, and Kevin McBride

2003 Indiantown (1760–1805): Survey and Inventory of a Transitional Community. Report compiled for the National Park Service under Grant Agreement 09-00-NA-0901. Report on file at the Mashantucket Pequot Museum and Research Center.

Jones, Calvin
   1815   Travel Journal. Unpublished manuscript, Southern Historical Collection, University of North Carolina, Chapel Hill.

Jones, Siân
   1999   Historical Categories and the Praxis of Identity: The Interpretation of Ethnicity in Historical Archaeology. *In* Historical Archaeology: Back from the Edge. Pedro Paulo A. Funari, Martin Hall, and Siân Jones, eds. Pp. 219–232. London: Routledge.

Joyner, Charles
   2005   Foreword: A Peculiar Political Culture. *In* A New World Gentry: The Making of a Merchant and Planter Class in South Carolina, 1670–1770. Richard Waterhouse, ed. Pp.7–11. Charleston, SC: History Press.

Jurgelski, William M.
   2004   A New Plow in Old Ground: Cherokees, Whites, and Land in Western North Carolina, 1819 to 1829. Ph.D. dissertation, Department of Anthropology, University of Georgia, Athens.

Kellaway, William
   1962   The New England Company 1649–1776: Missionary Society to the American Indians. Westport, CT: Greenwood Press.

Kenmotsu, Nancy
   1990   Gunflints: A Study. Historical Archaeology 24(2):92–124.
   2000   Gunflints: A Study. *In* Approaches to Material Culture Research for Historical Archaeologists. David R. Brauner, comp. Pp. 340–372. California, PA: Society for Historical Archaeology.

Keyes, Charles F.
   1981   Introduction. *In* Ethnic Change. Charles F. Keyes, ed. Pp. 4–30. Seattle: University of Washington Press.

Keyser, James L.
   1987   A Lexicon for Historic Plains Indian Rock Art: Increasing Interpretive Potential. Plains Anthropologist 32(115):43–71.

Keyser, James L., and Michael A. Klassen
   2001   Plains Indian Rock Art. Seattle: University of Washington Press.

Keyser, James L., Russell L. Tanner, and David T. Vlcek
   2004   Pictures by the Seedskadee: A Preliminary Analysis of the Biographic Rock Art of the Green River Basin, Southwestern, Wyoming. Plains Anthropologist 49(190): 129–151.

Kidd, Kenneth E., and Martha Ann Kidd
   1970   A Classification System for Glass Beads for the Use of Field Archaeologists. Canadian Historic Sites: Occasional Papers in Archaeology and History 1:45–89. Ottawa: National Historic Sites Service.

King, J. C. H.
   1977   Smoking Pipes of the North American Indian. London: British Museum Publications.

King, J. W.
    1844   Letter to William Holland Thomas, December 12, 1844. *In* James W. Terrell papers, Duke Special Collections, Duke University, Durham, North Carolina.

Kinnaird, L., ed.
    1949   Spain in the Mississippi Valley, 1765–1794. 3 vols. Annual Report for the Year 1945. Washington, DC: American Historical Association.

Klinck, Carl, and James Talman
    1970   The Journal of Major John Norton, 1816. Toronto: Champlain Society.

Kopytoff, Igor
    1986   The Cultural Biography of Things: Commoditization as Process. *In* The Social Life of Things: Commodities in Cultural Perspective. Arjun Appadurai, ed. Pp. 64–94. Cambridge: Cambridge University Press.

Krauskopf, Frances, ed. and trans.
    1955   Ouiatanon Documents. Indiana Historical Society Publications 18. Indianapolis.

Lavender, David
    1992   De Soto, Coronado, Cabrillo: Explorers of the Northern Mystery. Division of Publications, National Park Service. Washington, DC: United States Department of the Interior.

Leath, Robert A., and Maurie D. McInnis
    1999   "To Blend Pleasure with Knowledge": The Cultural Odyssey of Charlestonians Abroad. *In* In Pursuit of Refinement: Charlestonians Abroad, 1740–1860. Maurie D. McInnis and Angela D. Mack, eds. Pp. 9–22. Columbia: University of South Carolina Press.

Lee, D. B.
    1998   A Social History of Caddoan Peoples: Cultural Adaptation and Persistence in a Native American Community. Ph.D. dissertation, Department of Anthropology, University of Oklahoma, Norman.

Leone, Mark P.
    1999   Ceramics from Annapolis, Maryland: A Measure of Time Routines and Work Discipline. New York: Kluwer Academic/Plenum Publishers.

Leone, Mark P., Parker B. Potter Jr., and Paul A. Shackel
    1987   Toward a Critical Archaeology. Current Anthropology 28(3):283–302.

Lewis, Kenneth E.
    1976   Camden: A Frontier Town in Eighteenth-Century South Carolina. Anthropological Studies No. 2, South Carolina Institute of Archaeology and Anthropology, University of South Carolina Press, Columbia.

Lightfoot, Kent G.
    1995   Culture Contact Studies: Redefining the Relationship between Prehistoric and Historical Archaeology. American Antiquity 60:199–217.
    2005   Indians, Missionaries, and Merchants: The Legacy of Colonial Encounters on the California Frontiers. Berkeley: University of California Press.
    2006   Missions, Furs, Gold and Manifest Destiny: Rethinking an Archaeology of Colonialism for Western North America. *In* Historical Archaeology. Martin Hall and Stephen Silliman, eds. Pp. 272–292. Malden, MA: Blackwell Publishing.

Lightfoot, Kent G., and Antoinette Martinez
  1995   Frontiers and Boundaries in Archaeological Perspective. Annual Review of Anthropology 24:471–492.
Lightfoot, Kent G., Antoinette Martinez, and Ann M. Schiff
  1998   Daily Practice and Material Culture in Pluralistic Social Settings: An Archaeological Study of Culture Change and Persistence from Fort Ross, California. American Antiquity 63:199–222.
Lightfoot, Kent G., Thomas A. Wake, and Ann M. Schiff
  1993   Native Responses to the Russian Mercantile Colony of Fort Ross, Northern California. Journal of Field Archaeology 20:159–175.
Lincoln, Bruce
  1989   Discourse and the Construction Society: Comparative Studies of Myth, Ritual, and Classification. Oxford: Oxford University Press.
Lindgren, James Michael
  1993   Preserving the Old Dominion. Charlottesville: University Press of Virginia.
Lindsay, Batterman
  1899   Kwelth-Elite, The Proud Slave. Overland Monthly, 2nd Series 33:534–539.
Linton, Ralph
  1924   Use of Tobacco Among Native North Americans. Anthropology Leaflet 15, Field Museum of Natural History, Chicago, Illinois.
Loendorf, Lawrence L., and Linda Olsen
  2003   The Tolar Petroglyph Site. American Indian Rock Art 29:1–10.
Lydon, Jane
  2006   Pacific Encounters, or Beyond the Islands of History. *In* Historical Archaeology. Martin Hall and Stephen W. Silliman, eds. Pp. 293–312. Malden, MA: Blackwell Publishing.
Mann, Rob
  2004   Smokescreens: Tobacco, Pipes, and the Transformational Power of Fur Trade Rituals. *In* Smoking and Culture: The Archaeology of Tobacco Pipes in Eastern North America. Sean M. Rafferty and Rob Mann, eds. Pp. 165–183. Knoxville: University of Tennessee Press.
  2007   "True Portraitures of the Indians, and of Their Own Peculiar Conceits of Dress": Discourses of Dress and Identity in the Great Lakes, 1830–1850. Historical Archaeology 41(1):37–52.
  2008   From Ethnogenesis to Ethnic Segmentation in the Wabash Valley: Constructing Identity and Houses in Great Lakes Fur Trade Society. International Journal of Historical Archaeology 12:319–337.
Marceaux, Paul Shawn
  2007   Recent Research on the Archaeological and Historical Evidence of the Hasinai. Journal of Northeast Texas Archaeology 26:82–98.
Margry, Pierre, ed.
  1876   Decouvertes et Establissements des Francais dans L'Ouest et dans le Sud de L'Ameri-
  –86   que Septentrionale, 1614–1754. Memoires et Documents Originaux. 6 vols. D. Jouant, Paris. Anonymous translation, Ohio Valley-Great Lakes Ethnohistory

Archives, Glenn A. Black Laboratory of Archaeology, Indiana University, Bloomington.

McBride, K. A., W. S. McBride, and D. Pollack, eds.
   1996   Historical Archaeology in Kentucky. Frankfort: Kentucky Heritage Council.

McClintock, Anne
   1995   Imperial Leather: Race, Gender, and Sexuality in the Colonial Conquest. London: Routledge.

McCrocklin, C.
   1993   Chipped Glass, Ceramics, and Axe Handles. Notes on Northeast Texas Archaeology 2:8–13.

McDowell, W. L., ed.
   1969   Documents Relating to Indian Affairs, 1754–1765. Columbia: South Carolina Department of Archives and History.

McLoughlin, William G.
   1990   Champions of the Cherokees: Evan and John B. Jones. Princeton: Princeton University Press.
   1992   Cherokee Renascence in the New Republic. Princeton: Princeton University Press.

McReynolds, Theresa E.
   2004   Catawba Population Dynamics during the Eighteenth and Nineteenth Centuries. North Carolina Archaeology 53:42–59.

Medsger, Oliver P.
   1966   Edible Wild Plants. New York: Macmillan.

Meltzer, David J.
   2006   Folsom: New Archaeological Investigations of a Classic Paleoindian Bison Kill. Berkeley: University of California Press.

Merrell, James H.
   1989   The Indians' New World: Catawbas and Their Neighbors from European Contact through the Era of Removal. Chapel Hill: University of North Carolina Press.

Michel, Francois Louis
   1916   Report of the Journey of Francois Louise Michel from Berne, Switzerland, to Virginia, October 2, 1701–December 1, 1702. W. J. Hinke, trans. Virginia Magazine of History and Biography 24(1):1–43, (2):113–141, (3):275–303.
   [1701
   –02]

Michigan Pioneer and Historical Society
   1905   Michigan Pioneer and Historical Society Collections, vol. 34. Lansing: Wynkoop Hallenbeck Crawford.

Miller, George
   1991a   Classification and Economic Scaling of 19th Century Ceramics. *In* Approaches to Material Culture Research for Historical Archaeologists. George L. Miller, Olive R. Jones, Lester A. Ross, and Teresita Majewski, comps. The Society for Historical Archaeology.
   1991b   A Revised Set of CC Index Values for Classification and Economic Scaling of English Ceramics from 1787 to 1880. Historical Archaeology 25(1):1–25.

Mills, Robert
    1826   Statistics of South Carolina. Charleston, SC: Hurlbut and Lloyd.
Mississippi Messenger
    1806   Mississippi Messenger (Natchez), September 30, 1806.
Moogk, Peter
    1975   Building a House in New France. Toronto: McClelland and Stewart.
Mooney, James
    1982   Myths of the Cherokee and Sacred Formulas of the Cherokees. Reproduction of 19th and 7th Annual Reports B.A.E. Nashville, TN: Charles and Randy Elder Booksellers.
Moore, David G.
    2002   Catawba Valley Mississippian: Ceramics, Chronology, and Catawba Indians. Tuscaloosa: The University of Alabama Press.
Moore, S. L.
    2006   Savage Frontier, Volume II, 1838–1839: Rangers, Riflemen, and Indian Wars in Texas. Denton: University of North Texas Press.
    2007   Savage Frontier, Volume III, 1840–1841: Rangers, Riflemen, and Indian Wars in Texas. Denton: University of North Texas Press.
Morris, E. A., K. L. Kvamme, N. T. Ohr, M. D. Metcalf, H. M. Davidson, R. E. Kainer, and R. J. Burgess
    1979   The Archaeology of the Boxelder Project: A Water Control Project in Larimer County North Central Colorado, 1972–1979. A report prepared for the United States Department of Interior Interagency Archaeological Services, Denver Heritage Conservation and Recreational Service Contract No. C3511(74).
Moses, L. G.
    1996   Wild West Shows and the Images of American Indians, 1883–1933. Albuquerque: University of New Mexico Press.
Mrozowski, Stephen, Grace Ziesing, and Mary Beaudry
    1996   Living on the Boott: Historical Archaeology at the Boott Mills, Boardinghouses, Lowell, Massachusetts. Amherst: University of Massachusetts Press.
Muller, Jon
    1997   Mississippian Political Economy. New York: Plenum Publishers.
Mullins, Paul
    1999   Race and Affluence: An Archaeology of African America and Consumer Culture. New York: Kluwer Academic/Plenum Publishers.
Nassaney, Michael
    2008   Identity Formation at a French Colonial Outpost in the North American Frontier. International Journal of Historical Archaeology 12:297–318.
Neighbours, K. E.
    1973   Indian Exodus: Texas Indian Affairs, 1835–1859. Quannah, TX: Nortex Offset Publications.
    1975   Robert Simpson Neighbors and the Texas Frontier, 1836–1859. Waco: Texian Press.

Newton, Cody
  2008   The Protohistoric Period in Northcentral Colorado: Analysis of the Lykins Valley Site (5LR263). Unpublished master's thesis, Department of Anthropology, Colorado State University.

Noël Hume, Ivor
  1969   A Guide to Artifacts of Colonial America. Reprint edition. Philadelphia: University of Pennsylvania Press.
  1982   Martin's Hundred. New York: Alfred A. Knopf.

Oates, S. B., ed.
  1963   Rip Ford's Texas. Austin: University of Texas Press.

Ohr, N. Ted, Kenneth L. Kvamme, and Elizabeth Ann Morris
  1979   The Lykins Valley Site (5LR263): A Stratified Locality on Boxelder Creek, Larimer County, Colorado. A report prepared for the United States Department of Interior Interagency Archaeological Services, Denver Heritage Conservation and Recreational Service Contract No. C3517(74).

Orser, Charles E.
  2004   Race and Practice in Archaeological Interpretation. Philadelphia: University of Pennsylvania Press.
  2007   The Archaeology of Race and Racialization in Historic America. Volume in the Series, The American Experience in Archaeological Perspective. Gainesville: University of Florida Press.

Otto, John
  1984   Cannon's Point Plantation, 1794–1860: Living Conditions and Status Patterns in the Old South. New York: Academic Press.

Parsons, M. L., J. E. Bruseth, J. Bagur, S. E. Goldborer, and C. McCrocklin
  2002   Finding Sha'chahdinnih (Timber Hill): The Last Village of the Kadohadacho in the Caddo Homeland. Archeological Reports Series No. 3. Texas Historical Commission, Austin.

Perdue, Theda
  1998   Cherokee Women: Gender and Culture Change, 1700–1835. Lincoln: University of Nebraska Press.

Perttula, Timothy K.
  1992   "The Caddo Nation": Archaeological and Ethnohistoric Perspectives. Austin: University of Texas Press.
  1994   French and Spanish Colonial Trade Policies and the Fur Trade among the Caddoan Indians of the Trans-Mississippi South. In The Fur Trade Revisited: Selected Papers of the Sixth North American Fur Trade Conference, Mackinac Island, Michigan, 1991. J. S. H. Brown, W. J. Eccles, and D. P. Heldman, eds. Pp. 71–91. Lansing: Michigan State University Press.
  2001   Three Mid-1800s Caddo Vessels from the Brazos Reserve. Journal of Northeast Texas Archaeology 14:31–36.
  2008   Archeological Investigations at the D'Ortolan Site (41NA299) and Other Late 18th Century to Early 20th Century Sites along Bayou Loco in Western Nacog-

doches County, Texas. Report of Investigations No. 63. Archeological & Environmental Consultants, LLC, Austin.

Perttula, Timothy K., D. B. Lee, and R. Cast
2008 The First People of the Red River: The Caddo before and after Freeman and Custis. *In* Freeman and Custis Red River Expedition of 1806: Two Hundred Years Later. F. C. Hardy, ed. Pp. 81–110. Bulletin of the Museum of Life Sciences, No. 14. Museum of Life Sciences, Louisiana State University, Shreveport.

Perttula, Timothy K., and T. Middlebrook
2007 Historic Caddo Archaeology: An Occasional Meeting of the East Texas Caddo Research Group, December 2–3, 2006, in Nacogdoches, Texas. Journal of Northeast Texas Archaeology 26:1–7.

Perttula, Timothy K., and B. Nelson
2006 Test Excavation at Three Caddo Sites at Mission Tejas State Park, Houston County, Texas. Report of Investigations No. 76. Archeological & Environmental Consultants, LLC, Austin.

Peterson, Guy L.
1974 Fort Vasquez: Fact and/or Fantasy? Unpublished master's thesis, Department of Anthropology, Colorado State University, Fort Collins.

Peterson, Jacqueline L.
1981 The People in Between: Indian-White Marriage and the Genesis of a *Métis* Society and Culture in the Great Lakes Region, 1680–1830. Ph.D. Dissertation, Department of History, University of Illinois at Chicago Circle.

Pettus, Louise
2005 Leasing Away a Nation: The Legacy of Catawba Indian Land Leases. Spartanburg, SC: Palmetto Conservation Foundation.

Phillips, Ruth B.
1995 Why Not Tourist Art? Significant Silences in Native American Museum Representations. *In* After Colonialism: Imperial Histories and Postcolonial Displacements. Gyan Prakash, ed. Pp. 98–125. Princeton: Princeton University Press.
1998 Trading Identities: The Souvenir in Native North American Art from the Northeast, 1700–1900. Seattle: University of Washington Press.

Plane, Mark R., and Daniel Ladu
2006 Catawba Pottery and Consumer Choice in South Carolina during the Revolutionary and Federal Periods. Paper presented at the 63rd annual meeting of the Southeastern Archaeological Conference, Little Rock, Arkansas.

Porter, George
1838 Letter to General Abraham Eustis, June 18, 1838. Correspondence of the Eastern Division Pertaining to Cherokee Removal, April–December 1838. Record Group 393, Microcopy 1475, United States National Archives and Records Administration, Washington, DC.

Powell, John A.
1843 Testimony on Behalf of the Spoliation Claim of John and Elizabeth Welch. File 687, Records of the Fourth Board of Cherokee Commissioners, 1846–1847. Re-

cord Group 75, United States National Archives and Records Administration, Washington, DC.

Quaife, Milo M.
 1921   Fort Wayne in 1790. Indiana Historical Society Publications 7(7):293–361.
 1928   The John Askin Papers, vol. 1:1747–1795. Detroit: Detroit Library Commission.

Rabinow, Paul
 1984   Introduction. *In* The Foucault Reader. Paul Rabinow, ed. Pp. 3–30. New York: Pantheon Books.

Raibmon, Paige
 2005   Authentic Indians: Episodes of Encounter from the Late-Nineteenth-Century Northwest Coast. Durham, NC: Duke University Press.

Ramsay, John
 1947   American Potters and Pottery. New York: Tudor Publishing Company.

Rao, Aparna, ed.
 1987   The Concept of Peripatetics: An Introduction. *In* The Other Nomads: Peripatetic Minorities in Cross-Cultural Perspective. Pp. 1–34. Kölner Ethnologische Mitteilungen; Bd. 8. Böhlau Verlag GmbH & Cie, Köln.

Ray, Arthur J.
 1974   Indians in the Fur Trade: Their Role as Hunters, Trappers and Middlemen in the Lands Southwest of Hudson Bay 1660–1870. Toronto: University of Toronto Press.

Riggs, Brett H.
 1996   Removal Period Cherokee Households and Communities in Southwestern North Carolina (1835–1838). Final report of the Cherokee Homestead Project, submitted to the North Carolina State Historic Preservation Office, Division of Archives and History, Department of Cultural Resources, Raleigh, North Carolina.
 1999   Removal Period Cherokee Households in Southwestern North Carolina: Material Perspectives on Ethnicity and Cultural Differentiation. Unpublished Ph.D. dissertation, University of Tennessee, Knoxville. University Microfilms, Ann Arbor, Michigan.
 2000   Prehistoric and Historic Native American Artifacts at 31CE338. *In* Archaeological Data Recovery at the McCombs Slave Quarter Site (31CE338) Cherokee County, North Carolina. Scott Shumate, Patti Evans-Shumate, and Larry Kimball, eds. Appalachian State University Laboratories of Archaeological Science Technical Report. Manuscript submitted to the North Carolina Department of Transportation, Raleigh.

Riggs, Brett H., Stephen R. P. Davis, and Mark R. Plane
 2006   Catawba Pottery from the Post-Revolutionary Era: A View from the Source. North Carolina Archaeology 55:60–88.

Riggs, Brett H., Scott Shumate, and Patti Evans-Shumate
 1998   An Archaeological Survey of the Ferguson Farm, Swain County, North Carolina. Manuscript on file, Archaeology Branch, North Carolina Division of Archives and History, Raleigh.

2001 Archaeological Data Recovery at 31SW365 in the Below Pool Area of the Proposed Lemmons Branch Boat Ramp, Fontana Reservoir, Swain County, North Carolina. Manuscript submitted to the Tennessee Valley Authority, Norris, Tennessee.

Robertson, R. G.
1999 Competitive Struggle: America's Western Fur Trading Posts, 1764–1865. Boise, ID: Tamarack Books.

Robertson, William Spence, ed.
1928 The Diary of Francesco De Miranda: Tour of the United States, 1783–1784. New York: Hispanic Society of America.

Rogers, J. Daniel
1990 Objects of Change: The Archaeology and History of Arikara Contact with Europeans. Washington, DC: Smithsonian Institution Press.

Rothschild, Nan A.
2003 Colonial Encounters in a Native American Landscape: The Spanish and Dutch in North America. Washington, DC: Smithsonian Books.

Russell, Mattie
1956 William Holland Thomas, White Chief of the Cherokees. Ph.D. dissertation, Duke University, Durham, North Carolina.

Said, Edward W.
1978 Orientalism. New York: Vintage Books.
1993 Culture and Imperialism. New York: Vintage Books.

Sanchez, J. M.
1926 A Trip to Texas in 1828. C. E. Castaneda, trans. Southwestern Historical Quarterly 29(4):249–288.

Saunt, Claudio
1999 A New Order of Things: Property, Power, and the Transformation of the Creek Indians, 1733–1816. Cambridge: Cambridge University Press.

Scaife, H. Lewis
1930 History and Condition of the Catawba Indians. Indian Rights Association Pub-
[1898] lications, 2nd series, no. 31, Philadelphia.

Scheiber, Laura L.
1994 A Probable Early Nineteenth Century Crow Burial: The Pitchfork Rockshelter Reexamined. Plains Anthropologist 39(147):37–51.
2006 The Late Prehistoric on the High Plains of Western Kansas: High Plains Upper Republican and Dismal River. In Kansas Archaeology. Robert J. Hoard and William E. Banks, eds. Pp. 133–150. Lawrence: University Press of Kansas.

Schoolcraft, H. R.
1851 Historical and Statistical Information Respecting the History, Condition and
–57 Prospects of the Indian Tribes of the United States. 6 vols. Philadelphia.

Schroeder, Albert H.
1962 A Re-analysis of the Routes of Coronado and Oñate into the Plains in 1541 and 1601. Plains Anthropologist 7(15):2–23.

Schurr, Mark
 2006   Untangling Removal Period Archaeology: The Complexity of Potawatomi Sites. Midcontinental Journal of Archaeology 31(1):5–19.

Scott, Edwin J.
 1884   Random Recollections of a Long Life. Columbia, SC: Charles A. Calvo Press.

Scott, Elizabeth, ed.
 1994   Those of Little Note: Gender, Race, and Class in Historical Archaeology. Tucson: University of Arizona Press.

Sellers, Charles
 1991   The Market Revolution: Jacksonian America, 1815–1846. Oxford: Oxford University Press.

Setzler, Frank, and Jesse Jennings
 1941   Peachtree Mound and Village Site. Bureau of American Ethnology, Bulletin 131, Washington, DC.

Shackel, Paul
 1996   Culture Change and the New Technology: An Archaeology of the Early American Industrial Era. New York: Plenum Press.

Shackley, M. Steven
 2005   Obsidian: Geology and Archaeology in the North American Southwest. Tucson: University of Arizona Press.

Shumate, M. Scott, Patti Evans-Shumate, and Larry R. Kimball
 2000   Archaeological Data Recovery at the McCombs Slave Quarter Site (31CE338), Cherokee County, North Carolina. Final report submitted to the Federal Highway Administration and the North Carolina Department of Transportation.

Siler, David
 1972   The Eastern Cherokee: A Census of the Cherokee Nation in North Carolina,
 [1851] Tennessee, Alabama, and Georgia in 1851. Cottonport, LA: Polyanthos.

Silliman, Stephen W.
 2005   Culture Contact or Colonialism? Challenges in the Archaeology of Native North America. American Antiquity 70(1):55–74.
 2006   Struggling with Labor, Working with Identities. *In* Historical Archaeology. Martin Hall and Stephen W. Silliman, eds. Pp. 147–166. Malden, MA: Blackwell Publishing.

Simmel, Georg
 1978   The Philosophy of Money. London: Routledge.
 [1907]

Simms, William Gilmore
 2003a Caloya; or, the Loves of the Driver. *In* An Early and Strong Sympathy: The Indian
 [1841] Writings of William Gilmore Simms. John Caldwell Guilds and Charles Hudson, eds. Pp. 218–273. Columbia: University of South Carolina Press.
 2003b North American Indians. *In* An Early and Strong Sympathy: The Indian Writings
 [1828] of William Gilmore Simms. John Caldwell Guilds and Charles Hudson, eds. Pp. 7–19. Columbia: University of South Carolina Press.
 2003c Sketches of Indian Character No. 1. *In* An Early and Strong Sympathy: The In-

[1835] dian Writings of William Gilmore Simms. John Caldwell Guilds and Charles Hudson, eds. Pp. 25–34. Columbia: University of South Carolina Press.

Singleton, Theresa
   1980   The Archaeology of Afro-American Slavery in Coastal Georgia: A Perception of Slave Household and Community Patterns. Ph.D. dissertation, University of Florida, Gainesville.
   1985   The Archaeology of Slavery and Plantation Life. Orlando, FL: Academic Press.
   1996   The Archaeology of Slave Life. Walnut Creek, CA: Alta Mira Press, Walnut Creek.
   2004   The Archaeology of African American Life. Washington, DC: Smithsonian Books.

Singleton, Theresa, and Mark Bograd
   1995   The Archaeology of the African Diaspora in the Americas. Glassboro, NJ: Society for Historical Archaeology.

Skinner, Ellen
   1996   Women and the National Experience: Primary Sources in American History. New York: Addison-Wesley Educational Publishers.

Sleeper-Smith, Susan
   2001   Indian Women and French Men: Rethinking Cultural Encounter in the Western Great Lakes. Amherst: University of Massachusetts Press.

Smith, F. T.
   1991   The Kadohadacho Indians and the Louisiana-Texas Frontier, 1803–1815. Southwestern Historical Quarterly 95(2):176–204.
   1995   The Caddo Indians: Tribes at the Convergence of Empires, 1542–1854. College Station: Texas A&M University Press.
   2005   From Dominance to Disappearance: The Indians of Texas and the Near Southwest, 1786–1859. Lincoln: University of Nebraska Press.

Smith, G. Hubert
   1980   The Expeditions of the La Vérendryes in the Northern Plains, 1738–43. W. Raymond Wood, ed. Lincoln: University of Nebraska Press.

Smith, William Henry, ed.
   1882   The St. Clair papers: The Life and Public Services of Arthur St. Clair, Soldier of the Revolutionary War, President of the Continental Congress, and Governor of the North-Western Territory, with His Correspondence and Other Papers. 2 vols. Cincinnati, OH: Robert Clarke and Co.

Smyth, John Ferdinand
   1784   A Tour in the United States of America. London: G. Robinson, J. Robson, and J. Sewell.

Stein, Gil, ed.
   2005   Introduction: The Comparative Archaeology of Colonial Encounters. In The Archaeology of Colonial Encounters: Comparative Perspectives. Pp. 3–32. Santa Fe: School of American Research Press.

Stokes, Melvyn
   1996   Introduction. In The Market Revolution in America: Social, Political, and Religious Expressions, 1800–1880. Melvyn Stokes and Stephen Conway, eds. Pp. 1–20. Charlottesville: University Press of Virginia.

Stone, Lyle M.
 1974 Fort Michilimackinac, 1715–1781: An Archaeological Perspective in the Revolutionary Frontier. Publications of The Museum, Michigan State University, East Lansing.

Story, D. A., ed.
 1995 The Deshazo Site, Nacogdoches County, Texas, Vol. 2: Artifacts of Native Manufacture. Studies in Archeology 21. Texas Archeological Research Laboratory, University of Texas, Austin.

Strezewski, Michael, James R. Jones III, and Dorothea McCullough
 2006 Archaeological Investigations at Site 12-T-59 and Two Other Locations in Prophetstown State Park, Tippecanoe County, Indiana. Indiana University-Purdue University Fort Wayne Archaeological Survey, Reports of Investigations 513. Report submitted to the Indiana Department of Natural Resources, Division of Historic Preservation and Archaeology, Indianapolis.

Strezewski, Michael, Robert G. McCullough, Dorothea McCullough, Craig Arnold, and Josh Wells
 2007 Report of the 2006 Archaeological Investigations at Kethtippecanunk (12-T-59), Tippecanoe County, Indiana. Indiana University-Purdue University Fort Wayne Archaeological Survey, Reports of Investigations 703. Report submitted to the Indiana Department of Natural Resources, Division of Historic Preservation and Archaeology, Indianapolis.

Swanton, J. R.
 1942 Source Material on the History and Ethnology of the Caddo Indians. Bulletin 132. Bureau of American Ethnology, Smithsonian Institution, Washington, DC.

Tanner, Helen Hornbeck.
 1987 Atlas of Great Lakes Indian History. Norman: University of Oklahoma Press.

Tarlow, Sarah
 1999 Strangely Familiar. *In* The Familiar Past? Archaeologies of Later Historical Britain. Sarah Tarlow and Susie West, eds. Pp. 263–272. London: Routledge.

Thomas, Alfred Barnaby
 1935 After Coronado: Spanish Exploration Northeast of New Mexico, 1696–1727. Norman: University of Oklahoma Press.

Thomas, David H.
 1978 Arrowheads and Atlatl Darts: How the Stones Got the Shaft. American Antiquity 43(3):461–472.

Thomas, Robert
 1958 Cherokee Values and World View. Manuscript on file, North Carolina Collection, University of North Carolina, Chapel Hill.

Thomas, William Holland
 1839 Accounts of Indebtedness, 1839–1842, Murphy, Cherokee County, North Caro-
 –42 lina Ledger book L-3863, William Holland Thomas papers. Duke Special Collections, Duke University, Durham, North Carolina.
 1840 Census of the North Carolina Cherokees 1840. Manuscript copy in Box 1, un-

bound papers, William Holland Thomas papers, Duke Special Collections, Duke University, Durham, North Carolina.

Tieszen, Larry L., Karl Reinhardt, and D. Forshoe
  1997 Appendix C. Stable Isotopes in the Central and Northern Great Plains. *In* Bioarchaeology of the North Central United States. D. Owsley and J. Rose, eds. Pp. 329–336. Arkansas Archaeological Survey Research Series 49.

Tiller, J.
  2007 The Shreveport Caddo, 1835–1838. Journal of Northeast Texas Archaeology 26:159–167.
  2008 Was Timber Hill the Last Caddo Village in the Caddo Homeland? Caddo Archeology Journal 18:11–21.

Travis, Lauri
  1988 An Archaeological Survey in the Plains-Foothills Ecotone, Northern Colorado. Plains Anthropologist 33(120):171–186.

Trigger, Bruce G.
  1995 Romanticism, Nationalism, and Archaeology. *In* Nationalism, Politics, and the Practice of Archaeology. P. L. Kohl and C. Fawcett, eds. Pp. 263–279. London: Routledge.

Trubowitz, Neal L.
  1992a Native Americans and French on the Central Wabash. *In* Calumet and Fleur-de-Lys: Archaeology of Indian and French Contact in the Midcontinent. John A. Walthall and Thomas E. Emerson, eds. Pp. 241–264. Washington, DC: Smithsonian Institution Press.
  1992b Thanks, But We Prefer to Smoke Our Own: Pipes in the Great Lakes-Riverine Region During the Eighteenth Century. *In* Proceedings of the 1989 Smoking Pipe Conference: Selected Papers. Charles F. Hayes III, ed. Pp. 97–102. Rochester, NY: Rochester Museum and Science Center.

Tuross, Noreen, and Marilyn L. Fogel
  1994 Stable Isotope Analysis and Subsistence Patterns at the Sully Site, South Dakota. *In* Skeletal Biology of the Plains: Migration, Warfare, Health, and Subsistence. D. W. Owsley and R. Jantz, eds. Pp. 283–289. Washington, DC: Smithsonian Institution Press.

Usner, Daniel H., Jr.
  1992 Indians, Settlers, & Slaves in a Frontier Exchange Economy: The Lower Mississippi Valley before 1783. Chapel Hill: University of North Carolina Press.
  1998 American Indians in the Lower Mississippi Valley: Social and Economic Histories. Lincoln: University of Nebraska Press.

Van Dommelen, Peter
  2005 Colonial Interactions and Hybrid Practices. *In* The Archaeology of Colonial Encounters: Comparative Perspectives. Gil J. Stein, ed. Pp. 109–141. Santa Fe: School of American Research Press.

Van Gennep, Arnold
  1960   The Rites of Passage. Monika Vizedom and Gabrielle Caffee, trans. Chicago:
  [1909] University of Chicago Press.

Wagner, Mark J.
   2006   "He is Worst Than the [Shawnee] Prophet": The Archaeology of Nativism Among the Early Nineteenth Century Potawatomi of Illinois. Midcontinental Journal of Archaeology 31(1):89–116.

Wagner, Mark J., Terrance J. Martin, Lee A. Newsom, and Kathryn E. Parker
   2001   The Windrose Site: An Early Nineteenth-Century Potawatomi Settlement in the Kankakee River Valley of Northeastern Illinois. Reports of Investigations 56. Springfield: Illinois State Museum.

Ward, Trawick H., and R. P. Stephen Davis Jr.
   1999   Time Before History: The Archaeology of North Carolina. Chapel Hill: University of North Carolina Press.

Waterhouse, Richard
   2005   A New World Gentry: The Making of a Merchant and Planter Class in South Carolina, 1670–1770. Charleston, SC: History Press.

Watrous, Ansel
   1911   History of Larimer County Colorado, 1911. Fort Collins: Courier Printing and Publishing Company.

Watson, Elkanah
   1856   Men and Times of the Revolution: Memoirs of Elkanah Watson, Including Jour-
   [1785] nals of Travels in Europe and America, From 1777–1842. Winslow C. Watson, ed. New York: Dana and Company.

Watson, Harry L.
   1996   Slavery and Development in a Dual Economy: The South and the Market Revolution. *In* The Market Revolution in America: Social, Political, and Religious Expressions, 1800–1880. Melvyn Stokes and Stephen Conway, eds. Pp. 43–73. Charlottesville: University Press of Virginia.

Weber, David J.
   1992   The Spanish Frontier in North America. New Haven: Yale University Press.

Weber, Max
   1968   Economy and Society: An Outline of Interpretive Sociology. Guenther Roth and
   [1922] Claus Wittich, eds. New York: Bedminister Press.

Welch, John
   1843   Claim for spoliation of property. File 431, Records of the Fourth Board of Cherokee Commissioners, 1838–1844, Record Group 75, United States National Archives and Records Administration, Washington, DC.

Welch, William, and Nimrod Jarrett
   1838   Valuations of Cherokee Property in North Carolina. Manuscript, Record Group 75, United States National Archives and Records Administration, Washington, DC.

Welter, Barbara
   1966   The Cult of True Womanhood, 1820–1860. American Quarterly 18:151–175.

West, George A.
   1934   Tobacco, Pipes, and Smoking Customs of the American Indians. Bulletin of the Public Museum of the City of Milwaukee, Milwaukee, Wisconsin.

References

Wheaton, Thomas, Amy Friedlander, and Patrick Garrow
   1983   Yaughan and Curriboo Plantations: Studies in Afro-American Archaeology. Marietta, GA: Soil Systems.

Wheeler, Robert C., Walter A. Kenyon, Alan R. Woolworth, and Douglas A. Birk
   1975   Voices from the Rapids: An Underwater Search for Fur Trade Artifacts, 1960–73. Minnesota Historical Archaeology Series No. 3. St. Paul: Minnesota Historical Society.

Wheeler-Voegelin, Erminie, Emily J. Blasingham, and Dorothy R. Libby
   1974   Miami, Wea, and Eel-River Indians of Southern Indiana: An Anthropological Report on the Miami, Wea, and Eel-River Indians. New York: Garland.

White, Richard
   1991   The Middle Ground: Indians, Empires, and Republics in the Great Lakes Region, 1650–1815. Cambridge: Cambridge University Press.

Wilkie, Laurie A.
   2000   Creating Freedom: Material Culture and African American Identity at Oakley Plantation, Louisiana. Baton Rouge: Louisiana State University Press.

Wilkie, Laurie A., and Kevin M. Bartoy
   2000   A Critical Archaeology Revisited. Current Anthropology 41(5):747–776.

Wishart, David J.
   1979   The Fur Trade of the American West 1807–1840. Lincoln: University of Nebraska Press.

Witthoft, John
   1949   Stone Pipes of the Historic Cherokee. Southern Indian Studies 1:43–63.
   1966   A History of Gunflints. Pennsylvania Archaeologist 36(1–2):12–49.

Wolf, Eric R.
   1982   Europe and the People without History. Berkeley: University of California Press.

Young, Robert J. C.
   1995   Colonial Desire: Hybridity in Theory, Culture, and Race. London: Routledge.

Zug, Charles, III
   1986   Turners and Burners: The Folk Potters of North Carolina. Chapel Hill: University of North Carolina Press.

Contributors

Lance Greene is assistant professor of anthropology at American University in Washington, DC. His research focuses on 19th-century Cherokee archaeology in southwestern North Carolina.

P. Shawn Marceaux is a graduate student working on his doctorate in the Department of Anthropology at the University of Texas at Austin. His dissertation research focuses on the archaeology and archival records related to the American Indian–European experience at the time of initial contact through the missionization process. It specifically addresses how attributes of ceramic style and technology correlate with sites in the presumed locations of the Hasinai Caddo in east Texas. He has also coauthored "Hightower Anthropomorphic Marine Shell Gorgets and Duck River Sword-Form Flint Bifaces: Middle Mississippian Ritual Regalia in the Southern Appalachians" in *Southeastern Ceremonial Complex: Chronology, Content, Context*, edited by Adam King.

Cody Newton is a doctoral candidate in the Department of Anthropology at the University of Colorado in Boulder. He is currently researching 18th-century equestrian Indian groups on the western Great Plains.

Timothy K. Perttula received his Ph.D. in anthropology from the University of Washington in 1989. He has spent more than 30 years studying Caddo archaeology and ethnohistory, and after working for universities in Missouri and Texas, the National Park Service, the Advisory Council on Historic Preservation, and the Texas Historical Commission, he has been since 1996 the manager of Archeological & Environmental Consultants, LLC (Austin, Texas). He also serves as the Tribal Archaeological Consultant for the Caddo Nation of Oklahoma. Major publications include "*The Caddo Nation*": *Archaeological and Ethnohistoric Perspectives*, *The Prehistory of Texas*, and various articles on Caddo topics in the *Journal of Archaeological Research*, *Plains Anthropologist*, *American Antiquity*, and *Southeastern Archaeology*.

Mark R. Plane is a doctoral candidate in the Department of Anthropology at the University of North Carolina, Chapel Hill. His research on Catawba ceramic production has appeared in *North Carolina Archaeology*.

Michael Strezewski is assistant professor of anthropology at the University of Southern Indiana. He has published several articles and reports on Late Prehistoric and Historic American Indian peoples of Indiana and Illinois.

Index

agency, ix, 7–9, 11, 18, 33
agriculture, 26, 47, 53
Ais Indians, 85–86, 88
Alabama-Coushatta Indians, 83
Americans: and Caddo, 82–83, 86–88, 92, 96; exploration, 69; identity, 54–56; settlers, 21–22
Arapaho Indians, 2, 68, 70
architectural debris, 24, 25
Askin, John, 27
Atkin, Edmond, 37

beads, glass, 42, 68, 73, 77, 87–89, 91, 92
British, 5, 16, 21, 27, 28, 31, 46, 77; army, 45; expansionism, 82; government, 22; trade and traders, 2, 22, 26, 36, 37
Burnett, William, 27

Cache la Poudre River, 68, 69
caddi, 94, 95
Caddo Indians, 2, 17, 18, 80–97. *See also* identity; Removal
Camden (Pine Tree Hill), South Carolina, 37, 42
Canadiens. *See* French
capitalism, 7; archaeology of, 5
Catawba Indians, 1, 15, 16, 33, 34, 36–52; and battle, 15, 16, 34, 36, 37; and itinerancy, 16, 40, 43; leasing land, 1, 34, 39, 48; pipes, 16, 42–46; as slave catchers, 34, 38. *See also* identity; Nassaw Town; New Town; Old Town
Catawba River, 3
cellar pit, 22, 42, 59, 60, 62, 63, 65
ceramics, 1, 12, 16, 29, 30, 40, 42, 44–46, 59, 64, 89, 91, 92, 94; analysis of, 60–62; and class, 60; and ethnicity, 45, 46. *See also* colonoware; minimum number of vessels

Charleston, South Carolina, 1, 38, 40, 42, 49
Cherokee Indians, 1, 2, 8, 14, 16–17, 39, 48, 52, 53–59, 63–66, 70, 83; Cherokee Nation, 9, 53–57; Harmony Ethic of, 10; pipes, 63, 64. *See also* Removal
Cheyenne Indians, 2, 68, 70, 78, 79
Choctaw Indians, 2, 83, 96
Clark, William, 22
class (socio-economic), 8, 10, 14, 49; and use of whiteware, 60
classism, 12
coalescence, 17, 18, 68, 83, 95
colonialism, 5, 16, 33, 34, 36; American, 5, 6; and culture contact, 7, 8; and indigenous populations, 8
colonoware, 16, 39–42, 44
Comanche Indians, 68, 70, 78, 79
commodities and commoditization, 1, 2, 6, 11, 12, 18, 45; and gift exchange, x, 12
communities: traditional, 2, 3, 16, 17, 56–58, 66
consumption, 11, 12, 17
Creoles. *See* French
Currey, Benjamin, 55

Dearborn, Henry, 88
Deaver, Reuben, 55
deerskin trade, 6, 15, 16, 38, 51, 94
Dehahuit, 83, 94–96
Delaware Indians, 83
Detroit, 22–24, 26–28, 31
discourse, 34; on Indians, 16, 34–36, 46–52

Edisto River, 49
epidemic disease, 17, 18, 36, 37, 67, 69, 82, 94, 96. *See also* smallpox
ethnic soldiers, 36, 51–52
ethnicity, 13–15. *See also* identity

exchange, 3, 11, 12, 16, 25, 26, 87, 95; and gifts, x, 10, 12, 25, 87; market, 48

faunal remains, 65, 71, 73, 75, 76
femme covert, 58
firearms, 28, 29, 42, 73, 75, 77, 88, 91–92
fishing, 36, 47, 48, 51
floral remains, 65
foodways: traditional, 65, 91
foraging, 47
Fort Jackson, 68
Fort Mackinac, 27
Fort Montgomery, 56
Fort Ouiatenon, 21, 22
Fort Uncompahgre, 68
Freemasonry, 31
French, x, 5, 15, 20–23, 28, 36, 68, 77, 80, 82, 83, 87, 95; *Canadiens*, 15, 19, 28; Creoles, 87–88; culture, 19; trade and traders, 2, 21–22, 25–26, 28, 31, 69–70, 79, 82, 85, 87
French and Indian War, 28, 82
fur trade, 2, 19, 21, 22, 25–28, 31, 68, 78

gathering, 65
gender, 8, 10, 14, 63, 96
goods, x; consumer, 5, 12, 89; trade, 17, 27, 28, 38, 68, 70, 73, 78–79, 88–89, 92
Great Lakes, 19, 21, 26, 27, 37
Great Plains, 67–71, 76–79
Gros Ventre Indians, 68

Hasinai Indians, 80, 81, 83, 84, 86–88, 95
Hawkins-Sourjohn site, 62, 64
hearths, 73
Hindman, Thomas, 57, 58
historical archaeology, 1, 6–9, 15, 18; and ethnicity, 13
horticulture, 26
hunting, 16, 17, 27, 34, 36, 47, 48, 51, 68, 75, 76, 79
Hutchison, David, 47, 48
hybridity, 15

Illiniwek Indians, 29
identity, ix, xi, 1, 10–12, 15, 17, 33; Caddo, 94–96; Catawba, 16, 34, 36, 45, 46, 52; cross-cultural, 30; cultural, 65, 94; ethnic, 3, 14, 15, 21, 23, 28, 33, 45, 46, 48, 63, 73, 91; European, 30; formation of, 15, 16, 25, 46; Indian, 8, 9–12, 28, 29, 31, 36, 79; markers of, 11, 45; marketing of, 46; traditional, 28–29, 59; racial, 14, 33. See also *métis*
itinerancy, 16, 33, 34, 36, 43

James, Edwin, 68

Kadohadacho Indians, 18, 80, 81, 83, 85–87, 89–91, 94, 96
kaolin pipes, 30, 31, 42–46
Kentucky, 21; militia, 2, 21, 22
Kethtippecanunk, Indiana, 2, 15, 19–32; destruction of, 2, 22
Kickapoo Indians, 2, 21, 22, 83
King, J. W., 58
King Hagler, 37
Kiowa Indians, 2, 68, 70
Knox, Henry, 22

Lamar, Mirabeau, 86
land leases, 1, 39, 47
Lipan Apache Indians, 88
lithic analysis, 17, 71, 73, 75
Little Tennessee River, 56
livestock, 1, 4, 21, 23, 26, 53, 56, 57, 59, 65, 70, 87, 88, 94
Lykins Valley, 17, 67–71, 75, 77, 79; site, 17, 67–69, 71–72, 74, 77–79

Mascouten Indians, 21, 22
market economy, 3–6 ; and Cherokees, 48; and Indian identity, 9, 10, 16, 28; and the frontier, 87; Indian involvement in, 1, 2, 15, 51; and Kethtippecanunk, 26
material culture, xi ; and acculturation, 6; and ethnicity, 13, 15, 17, 63, 65; and gender, 63; and market expansion, 5; selective adoption by Indians, 1, 8, 17, 25, 73, 91–92; traditional, 29, 73
McCombs site, 60, 64
métis, 8, 28, 30, 48
Middle Caddo village site, 92
minimum number of vessels, 59
mobility, 5, 17, 36, 69

Nacogdoches Indians, 88
Nacogdoches, Texas, 82, 83, 87, 88, 92–94
Nassaw Town, North Carolina (Catawba), 40–44, 47

Index

Natchitoches Indians, 80, 81, 85, 87–89
New River, Sally, 50
New Town, North Carolina (Catawba), 40–48
North Carolina, 1, 3, 8, 16, 38, 49, 50–59, 62, 63, 65, 66. *See also* specific towns and cities

Ohio River, 21
Old Town, North Carolina (Catawba), 37, 40, 41, 42, 44, 46, 47
origin narratives, 14, 18, 83, 94

Pamunkey Indians, 44, 45
patron-client relation, 2, 57, 66
petroglyphs, 77
Piankashaw Indians, 21
pièces-sur-pièces construction, 15, 23
Pine Tree Hill, South Carolina. *See* Camden, South Carolina
pipes, smoking, 16, 25, 30, 31, 42–46, 63, 64; and commoditization, 1, 13, 16, 43, 45; and spiritual/ritual practices, 30; stone, 25, 30, 63, 64. *See also* Catawba: pipes; Cherokee: pipes; kaolin pipes
plant collecting, 65
population loss, 18, 34, 36–39, 96
postcolonial era, 5, 9; and Texas archaeology, 96
postcolonialism and postcolonial theory, 5, 7, 9, 33
Powell, John, 56, 57
Prophetstown State Park, 19

Qualla series ceramics, 64, 65

race, 6, 10, 13, 14; mixed, 17; and slavery, 7; vanishing, 1, 16, 35, 50–52
Red River, 80, 82, 83, 86, 88, 89
Removal, Indian, 1–2, 7, 35; Caddo, 86, 87, 97; Cherokee, 8, 16, 48, 53–59, 63–65
Revolutionary War, 1, 4, 6, 21, 27, 31, 47, 82
roasting pit, 15, 23, 29
Ross, John, 53

Sanders, Marcus, 52
Scott, Charles, 22
Seminole Indians, 53
Sha'chahdínnih (Caddo), 83, 89–90

shatter zone, 36
Shawnee Indians, 83
Shreveport, Louisiana, 86
Sibley, John, 88
Simms, William Gilmore, 41, 49, 50–52
slaves and slavery, 6, 7, 9, 16, 18, 36, 37–40, 42, 50, 53, 56, 59, 60, 65
smallpox, 21, 37, 40, 94
smudge pits, 47, 91
Smyth, John Ferdinand, 46, 47, 51
South Platte River, 68, 69
Spanish, x, 5, 68, 70, 71, 82, 83, 87, 88, 93–95; artifacts, 78, 79; colonies, 9; conquistadors, 52; *entradas*, 68; missions and missionaries, 9, 81, 82, 87, 91, 92, 95; traders, 82
stone working, 63, 64
Storage pits, 23, 29

Texas, 77, 80–83, 86–88, 92, 94–97; east, 2, 3, 80–83, 87–90, 92–93, 95–96
Texas Indians, 88
Timber Hill site, 91, 92, 96. See also *Sha'chahdínnih*
Tippecanoe River, 19, 22
Treaties of 1817 and 1819, 56
Treaty of New Echota, 53
Treaty of Paris, 82

utensils: analysis of, 62

Valley River, 56–59, 62, 65
Vincennes, Indiana, 21, 24, 27, 28
Virginia, 39, 44, 45

Wabash River, 3, 19, 21
warfare, 16, 36, 37; colonial era, 16, 34
Wea Indians, 2, 15, 19, 21, 22, 30
Welch cabin site, 59, 60–62
Welch, Elizabeth, 16, 55, 58
Welch, John, 16, 55–58, 63
Welch's Town, 57–59, 62–66
Western Turnpike, 59
Wilkinson, James, 22, 26
world systems theory, 9

Yatasi Indians, 86, 88